THE WILL POWER

FIGHTING / BREAKING
APPLICATIONS TECHNIQUES IN
SELF DEFENSE
FITNESS • PHILOSOPHY • CONDITIONING

MAURICE ELMALEM

BUDO INTERNATIONAL PUBLISHING CO

Budo International Publishing Co.
Main Office:
Andrés Mellado, 42
28015, Madrid, Spain
Tel.: (34) 91 897 8340. Fax: (34) 899 3319
budo@budointernational.com • www.budointernational.com

9 7 8 0 9 7 4 5 0 7 9 0 3

ISBN: 0-9745079-0-3
Edited by Martha Newman
Barbara Rogers
Ellen Rachlin

Jacket design by Maurice Elmalem

Publisher: Budo International Publishing Co.
Maurice Elmalem
The Will Power: fighting / breaking / self defense
applications by Maurice Elmalem and students assistants.
- 1st ed.

Includes hard cover, contents, index
ISBN: 0-9745079-0-3

Photographed and writing USA

Disclaimer:
This book is presented as a means of preserving special aspects of the martial arts heritage. The publisher nor author of this material cannot be responsible for any injury sustained during the performance of the techniques described, illustrated or photographed in this book. If techniques described in this book are properly mastered and executed the should cause no harm, however you should consult your doctor and an expert master of the martial art if you attempt any technique mentioned in this book.

Dedication

This book is dedicated to the spirit of the martial arts and the founders. To my Grandmaster Dr. Richard Chun for his encouragement to write this book. To Great Grand Master Aaron Banks who opened the doors of dreams and brought out the best in all martial artists. To my mother, God bless, for her encouragement and inspiration: "Hope is a good thing, good things never die." To my father the gentleman and to my wife and my children for their support, God bless. To all the martial artists who support its innovation of healthy life and soul. To God who gave me the strength, talent, and ideas to make my dreams come true.

"Martial Art is the innovation within ourselves."

Photographs by:

Lee Seuk Je
Maurice Elmalem
John Dentato
Silvia Cruz
Al Sussman
Andrew Shin
Allan Price
Ronnie Wright

Designed by:

Maurice Elmalem
Eddie Pearse
Silvia Cruz

Editors:

Martha Newman
Barbara Roger
Ellen Rachlin

Maurice Elmalem
The Will Power

Contents

The United States Taekwondo Association

220 EAST 86TH STREET, NEW YORK, N.Y. 10028 TEL: (212) 772-8918 • FAX: (212) 772-8919

23 January 2003

Dear Maurice,

Congratulations on your well-written book. It shows and tells the fundamental steps from your experience as a Six Time World Champion in martial arts. The way you tell the story is extraordinary and is easy to understand, starting with conditioning warm up. Step by step, kicking, free sparing and fighting are where you have supplied a great depth of information, including best techniques, philosophy and the truth from the heart on how to approach a fight, whether in competition or in the street. As I see it, only with your experience and knowledge in fighting will students of the martial arts learn what it takes to have the winning edge.

As your Grand Master, I have always been impressed with the way you teach, study the martial arts and, most important, execute the techniques. With great style and flair, even if danger was involved, you always took the chance to demonstrate well. The breaking section of the book explains step forms, breaking and application. No one can put it better. After witnessing some of your fighting and breaking competitions, the students can understand easily and do it themselves.

Maurice, you are a great inspiration to all the family of sports and martial arts. Movie Star Chuck Norris was right when he put the World Champion Belt on you at Madison Square Garden by saying, "You are a great champion."

I believe you are a great author. Your ideas are always bright and you put an architectural touch into the martial arts. I recommend students of the martial arts and non-martial artists to use this book, <u>The Will Power,</u> as a guide to learn how to perfect the art from basics to advanced.

Best wishes for your continued progress in the art of TaeKwonDo.

Yours Truly,

Grand Master Dr. Richard Chun

"ORIENTAL WORLD OF SELF-DEFENSE"

The Show That Made Marital Arts Into A Form of Entertainment

World's # One Martial Arts Show World Karate Magazine

Waldorf Astoria
Madison Square Garden
Studio 54
The Ritz
Nassau Coliseum
Meadowlands Arena
Long Beach Arena
Over 40 States in U.S.
Toured Europe & South America
ABC Wide World of Sports
NBC Sports World
CBS Sports Spectacular
HBO
Cablevision

Karate
Kung Fu
Judo
Ju Jitsu
Aiddo
Nin Jitsu
Kickboxing
Tae Kwon Do
Cap Lero
Stickfighting
Ketsugo
(Everything Goes)
Hapkido
World Championship's Team
Championships
Incredible Feats
Breaking, etc

My dear friend, World Champion:
Master Maurice Elmalem

I and millions around the world have seen many of your wins in fighting using the agility, speed, accuracy and power in those victories.

In the breaking segment of the book you show in detail, step by step, how to become a breaking champion, as you have proved over and over again by winning many a Grand championship in the breaking category at tournaments. Your book "The Will Power" provides the instructor as well as the student an opportunity to learn and prove their skills with great value of research. Maurice, you are a media phenomenon being on television, radio, newspaper, magazine, etc. Your latest experience being on Fox TV Guinness World Record Prime 2001 as the featured story, established a new world record: Time 2001 as the featured story, established a new world record: breaking 50 sheets of glass with shuto open knife hand, in 2002 Madrid Spain at Budo International Martial Arts Magazine Studio. You broke 100 sheets of glass with an elbow strike downward making it your 6th World Record. You are a 9th Degree Black Belt with world professional martial art organization, a master in Tae Kwon Do 6th Degree Black Belt in this book you teach the art of fighting and breaking in a well rounded service of self defense and an in-depth look of what martial arts is all about and how it helps you in all different areas. It is the one of its kind to have covered the most essential arts for training and learning.

You have genuinely given the reader the techniques and ideas that brought you to the top of the world: Madison Square Garden, Wide World of Sports, ABC, etc. The reader should follow your writings with diligent fervor and take advantage of such well proven experience and technique that turned you into a Martial Arts Master and a World Champion.

I have read many martial arts books and in good faith could not recommend any as I do this one by you, Master Elmalem. The reader certainly can use this book to develop oneself into a champion. Here is my favorite expression when someone asked me "How does one get to be in your events Great Grand Master Aaron Banks?" My answer has always been "practice, practice, practice!"

This Book is a must- can't wait for the next one to come out.
Bravo – Bravo - Bravo
World Champion Maurice Elmalem Greatest Martial Art Daredevil
The First in history The Glass Breaker of All Time
The Houdini of Martial Arts
World Champion in Fighting.

Sincerely yours,

Great Grand Master Aaron Banks
Founder of Oriental World
Of Self Defense.

GREAT GRAND MASTER AARON BANKS
P.O. Box 747771 Rego Park, New York 11374

INTRODUCTION

During thirty-two years of study in the martial arts, I have competed globally in more than seven hundred and fifty championships. I am often asked by spectators of all ages how I have achieved mastery in the martial arts skills of fighting and breaking. I have always believed in demonstrating my skills as transparently as possible so spectators can understand how the fighting and breaking occurs successfully. Martial arts are skills, not magic. Nonetheless, many people do not realize the philosophy and the strength one must hold to achieve complicated breaking techniques and win championship fights.

I wished to write this book to share my philosophy and training techniques with students of the martial arts. I hope that readers will find these chapters full of important information on how to improve their breaking and fighting skills, by developing all the facets of breaking and fighting, including the physical, spiritual and emotional disciplines. It is worthwhile for me to communicate my experiences in a book form. I hope that I will answer many of the questions I have been asked over the years, and believe within these answers students should find ways to improve their fighting and breaking skills.

I have experienced the easy way, the hard way and the hardest way to accomplish a given break. The well-executed break results in no harm to the martial artist. I will cover ways competitors can improve their fighting and breaking skills step by step, including training and conditioning of the mind, body and spirit. These results will enable one to break and fight better. Discipline and dedication are all these improvements take.

In top-level competitions, many spectators are silent, mesmerized by the spectacular breaking and fighting techniques. Many cheer. The attention is very helpful, but a standing ovation does not exclude the competitor's necessity to do everything right which includes having to maintain a good attitude, constant training, and split-second timing.

One begins with the basics and builds to a more advanced level. There are different grades of breaking and different levels of competition. The same holds true for fighting. My book will consider the easy as well as the advanced. It will speak to the juniors and the adults covering the beginning basics of breaking and fighting like a champion. Even the disabled can break. There are special training exercises the disabled may adapt to execute spectacular breaking techniques.

Today millions in the United States study or have studied the martial arts. This interest fuels movies, books, magazines, newspapers, commercials and TV shows giving the public more information and knowledge of the martial arts. In the 1988 Olympics in Korea and the 2000 Olympics in Australia there were amazing demonstrations of breaking skills. Fighting is now an Olympic sport.

I have always tried to give martial arts students all the information I could when they have sought me out to improve their skills and knowledge. My own skills developed through study, hard work and competition over many years and in many countries. And so this book is about proper training, necessary mindset and discipline. One's commitment to the martial arts is only the beginning. Success often means taking calculated risks. The first steps are meditation and discipline.

My Grand Master, Dr. Richard Chun, and students at my school have often asked why I have not written a book. I now have and it is my honor to teach some of what I have learned in the martial arts.

Martial Art is innovation within oneself.
Glory comes with winning.
If the fear is eliminated, relaxation, speed and power
will bring the win. Dreams are achieved only by
determination and strong will power.
Dreams are good for the mind and soul,
they keep us healthy and young with good spirit.
The risk takers are the ones to enrich all our lives everyday.

- Master Maurice Elmalem

HOW TO GET STARTED

This book outlines steps to create the power to break and fight no matter what level of expertise one has in the martial arts. This book covers conditioning techniques for the discipline of breaking and fighting. These techniques improve the body's reflexes, which in turn improve one's strength and power. There is a philosophy within this study which can be individualized for one's specific levels of athleticism. All practitioners will be tested and defined so that they will be better prepared to face an opponent, whether that opponent will be another human being or an inanimate object for breaking. The reader will be urged to learn to think ahead in preparation to do his or her personal best.

The development of power for fighting and breaking is interrelated. It will be easier to defend oneself in a fight because breaking will provide one with strength. Breaking is the ultimate test in the world of martial arts. To do it well, one must adjust his or her daily routine. Take it or leave it. The energizing sport of the martial arts keeps one young and trains one to aspire. This book will show how to achieve discipline within the philosophy of the martial arts.

NOTE

This book is presented as a means of preserving special aspects of the martial arts heritage. The publisher nor author cannot be responsible for any injury sustained during the performance of the techniques described, illustrated or photographed in this book. If techniques described in this book are properly mastered and executed, they should cause no harm; however, you should consult your doctor and an expert master of the martial arts if you attempt any technique mentioned in this book.

7 Time World Champion / Guinness World Record Holder

Breaking. The test of the mind, integrity, power, speed, focus, flexibility and coordination

Conditioning. Make it a part of survival - stay fit

High Jumping Front Kick

**Advanced Fighting
Techniques**

Section I

CONDITIONING

Conditioning - basic elements to a long and healthy life.

People fuss, people complain, people brag "If you don't love yourself you can't love anyone,"
Stay healthy.

CHAPTER 1

My Favorite Warm-up

Please consult a physician before beginning any exercise program.

I wear very light clothing: shorts, T-shirt, sneakers. If possible, I work out on a wooden floor.

Upper Body Warm- Up

In order to develop strength, speed and accuracy in any style of martial art, such as tae kwon do, kung fu, shodokan, tang sung du, etc., one needs to find a basic aerobic and strength training routine to condition the body for power and speed.

I suggest breathing exercises in between each exercise. Stand with palms open. Raise the arms above head, inhaling as you raise hands, then in a wide motion, push hands down toward the trunk of body and exhale. This releases the extra oxygen stored in the body while working out. Repeat this breathing exercise two times in between each exercise.

Neck & Elbow

a & b
Keep hands on the hips; bend head up and down for three counts gently with chin pointing towards the ceiling.

a

b

Shoulders

c, d
Raise left arm overhead then grab elbow with right arm and push back.

e
Raise right arm overhead then grab elbow with left arm and push back.

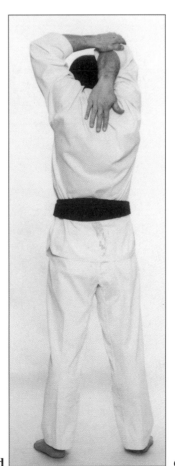

c

d

e

Neck Exercise

a Assume ready stance.
Both feet one step apart,
hands down fist lock.

b Ready stance. Put hands
on hips.

c Tilt head to the left for
four counts.

d Tilt head to the right for
four counts. Then circle
head in slow round
circular motions.

a

b

c

d

a

b

Shoulders

a Open arms shoulder height. Tight fist, stay in high stance.

b Bend arms shoulder height. Then circle the shoulders forward and back.

c Twist shoulders to the left in circular motion. Keep feet facing forward.

d Switch and twist shoulders to the right, in circular motion three times.

c

d

Arm and Shoulder Warm-up

a Bend right arm at shoulder height and with the left hand push backwards.

b Bend left arm at shoulder height and with the right hand push backwards while in high stand.

a

b

Lower Body Warm-up

c In preparation for the first lower body exercise, place feet shoulder width apart with feet parallel, bend forward at the hips and attempt to touch the floor. Hold the position without bouncing. This exercise stretches the legs in the hamstring area. After ten counts, return to a standing position with both hands supporting back hip area, bend backwards as far as possible without forcing the movement. Exhale for five counts. Resume standing position. Then bend forward, with the arms extended towards the floor. Keep the knees locked. If you cannot touch the floor, reach only as far as you can. Greater flexibility comes with practice. Reach towards the floor for two counts, return to a standing position, place the hands to support the hips and bend backward for two counts. Complete this exercise five times.

The next exercise begins in a standing position with the legs double shoulder width apart. Extend the left arm and reach towards the right foot and try to touch your head to the right knee. Hold for two counts. Exhale as you reach, inhale as you return to a standing position between stretches. Then, repeat to the otherside. Complete this stretch twice to each side. Keep knees locked.

d While bending forward grab legs with hands and pull head to knees.

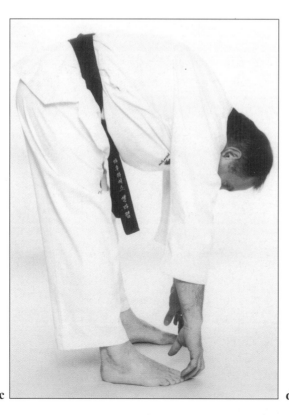

c

d

Back & Sides

a From normal stance, place feet shoulder width apart. Bend down half way. Place hands on knees, assuming a horse stance.

b From horse stance bring feet up, lock knees and repeat.

c Switch, extend right arm and reach toward the left foot. Hold for two counts.

d With legs double shoulder width apart, extend left arm toward right foot. Hold for two counts.

a Place left hand on left hip for support with your right hand open. Reach overhead and stretch left side two times. Make sure you do not move backwards or forwards.

b Place left arm over head while in normal stance. Push side way for three counts.

c Place left arm over head while in normal stance. Grab hands together and pull side way.

d Switch. Place right arm over head. Grab hands together and pull down to your left.

Leg Stretching

a From horse back stance, hands on the knees, bend left leg and extend right leg, lock knee with feet facing forward. Stay for two counts.

b Switch. Bend right leg with the support of hands on knee, lock left leg with foot facing forward. Stay for two counts.

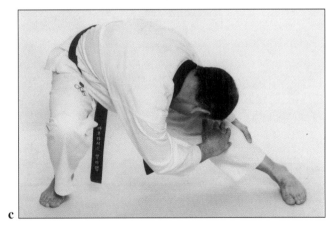

c Bend right leg halfway down, lock left leg with foot facing forward. Grab with both hands and pull, touching head to left knee.

d Switch. Bend left leg and repeat same to stretch other leg.

Leg Stretching

a

a Begin in standing position, legs double shoulder width apart, hands on both knees.

b Keep both feet facing forward with both hands on the floor. Extend legs further outwards.

b

c With both hands on the floor rotate upper body forward and backward in push up position. Exhale as you reach, inhale as you return to standing position between stretches.

d Extend the left arm and reach towards the left foot. Try to touch your head to left knee. Hold for two counts.

e Repeat same to right side. Complete this stretch twice to reach side. Keep knees locked.

c

d

e

Leg Stretching

a, b
Return to a side split-like position, legs wide apart with weight on the hands and heels, toes stretched upward towards ceiling. The hands provide a base of support and balance. Hold for three counts, and then slowly sit on the floor. Breathe - which in Korean sounds phonetically shoom-shē-gē. Take a deep breath and move the arms as described earlier.

a

c
Switch to left side. Hold to left side and repeat. Hold for five counts, breathe normal during execution of this stretch. Always exhale at the hardest point of the stretch and inhale at the loose point as your muscles relax. This releases the tension on the spine.

b

d
While sitting, lock knees. Grab right leg and pull upper body and head to reach right knee.

c

e
With fists, massage lower back by tapping back and forth. Then massage the back, using your fists to loosen the tension. Stay in the split position and stretch side to side. Try to touch the head to the knee. Do this exercise reaching two times to each side. On the second attempt, reach farther than on the first one. Repeat this exercise five times. Then, grasp the right ankle and attempt to touch head to the knee. Keep the knees locked, attempt to keep the spine straight. Hold for five counts on each side. Return to upright body position with the legs in side split position. Relax and shoom-shē-gē.

d

f
Massage the thigh muscles with fists by hitting the inside and outside of the thighs to relax the tensed muscles. Each leg should be massaged to relax the muscles. The beginner will sense most of the pain in the thigh area the next day after training. Gently shake the legs up and down, slapping the floor with the legs.

e

f

Legs and Lower Body

a Place the soles of your feet together, heels close to the body and knees bent in an open frog position. Bounce legs up and down 10 times.

b While sitting in split leg position, bring right hand over side-way stretch by pushing body and head to left side.

c Repeat same to right side, hold for two counts.

d With both legs in split position, grab both left and right ankles and pull body forward for three counts and repeat. Now return to standing position and shake legs sideways up and down to ease the tension on hips, thigh and leg muscles.

e In same frog position, lean forward and place the weight of the body on the shoulders. Pull forward and up to loosen back and leg muscles.

Legs and Lower Body

a Sit with left leg extended to left side. Bend right leg into left leg and extend position to 90 degrees. Grab left leg by ankle with both hands and pull body and head forward touching your knee. Raise up and repeat for three counts, do same stretch for right leg.

b From same position, raise both arms shoulder height. Bend arms and in a circular motion backwards and forwards, stretching back muscles and hip. Repeat for right side.

c Same position - lock right arm by your leg and with left arm resting on the floor twist body backward, stay in steady position for three counts. Repeat for left side.

Legs and Lower Body

a While sitting on floor extend left leg forward and grab heel of leg forward and grab heel of leg with right arm. Straighten the leg and bend by pulling it back as far as you can, repeat for three times.

b Switch and repeat same for left leg stretch.

c From same sitting position, grab both heels of right and left legs, and, in bending position, extend legs, pulling them up and back as far as possible. Keep balance with firm grip and lean forward. Repeat several times.

Neck Back and Shoulders

a Lie on your front, extend legs backward with instep flat against the floor. Place both arms by chest area with hands flat on floor. Straighten arms, raise head and shoulders up, lock your elbows.

b Twist to right. Hold for four counts. Repeat stretch for three times.

c Same position, twist head and neck to the left. Hold for three counts.

Floor Exercise

a

b

a, b
Lie back. Lift both legs while supporting yourself by placing both arms under buttocks. Push legs forward, bend backward. Repeat for five times.

c
Lift legs off the floor. Place the weight of the body on the shoulders and pick up your head. Split legs apart outward, bring back and forward. Repeat this exercise for five times.

c

d, e
Same position, cross legs with right leg on top and switch left leg on top.

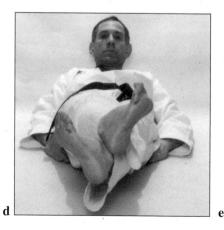

d

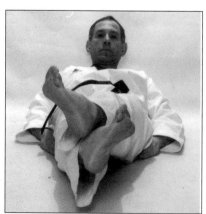

e

a

b

c

d

a Sit on the floor with both legs forward.

b Keep left leg in front of you. Place right leg behind with knee bent. Grab right leg and bounce leg up and down.

c Switch and do same stretch for left leg, keep body aligned.

d Upper and Lower Back
Sit with legs extended forward, pick up legs and roll back.

e Support back with both hands, split legs open, toes facing floor. Stay for three counts. It helps lower back, legs and shoulders for flexibility.

e

Feet and Legs

a

b

a, b

Sit with both legs extended forward. Put left leg on right leg in bending position. Stretch leg muscles by pushing with right hand against foot, fingers back and forth. Repeat and do same for right leg.

c, d

Sit on floor, both legs extended straight on the floor. With both hands pick up right leg with right hand grasping leg from inside and left hand grasping from the outside pull leg up to your head. Bring leg down and repeat. Switch and execute same for left leg.

c

d

Back and Leg Stretching

a With soles of feet facing up to the ceiling, support lower back with both hands and raise lower body up to use own weight for upper body stretch.

a

b

b Same position, both legs up. Maintain right leg up, align toe facing the ceiling, lower left leg down to reach the floor and support lower back with hand. Hold for three counts and switch to right leg.

c,d Sit with legs extended forward. Lift legs and roll backward in slow motion touching the floor. Hold for three counts then roll forward and repeat, supporting lower back with hands.

c

d

Wrist, Fingers and Hand Stretching

a Open Left Hand
Grab with right hand all fingers of left hand. Begin pressing fingers of left hand backwards as far as possible. Switch position. Raise left hand, face up and press left fingers with right hand downward to stretch back of wrist. Repeat same for right hand stretch.

b Wrist
Repeat facing the wrist upward. Grab right hand fingers in middle area, press right hand downward to stretch the outside part of the wrist. Repeat same for left hand.

c Side Wrist and Knuckles Stretching
Repeat as above sideways.

d Thumb Stretch
Press thumb with opposite hand downward and sideways. Repeat for both hands.

Power & Push Ups

a

b

a Position hands or knuckles flat on floor. Lie face down on the floor. Hands should be open and spaced at the point of shoulder, legs extended, with balls of the feet resting on floor.

b Raise body by straightening arms. Do not let buttocks sag. Keep weight towards the front of the body, drop down and push up slowly as many times as you can. Inhale as you go down, exhale as you push up.

Knuckle Push Ups
c, d
Repeat as above by raising left leg, push up and down, then switch. Place weight on knuckles.

e Correct fist. Use forefinger and middle knuckles.

c

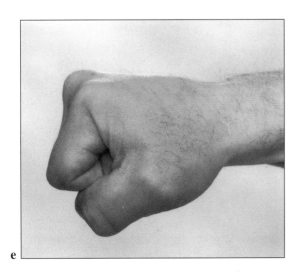

e

d

a

b

c

Finger Push Ups
a, b

Repeat exercise by doing same as knuckle push ups, placing body weight on fingertips of left and right hands.

Thumb Push Ups
c, d, e

Repeat as above. Place upper weight on thumbs, start with both legs bent resting on the knees, then slide legs back further as you progress to make sure you can maintain balance. Push up slowly.

d

e

Wrist push-ups

a

b

a, b Repeat as knuckle push up. Place wrist on floor, both legs bent resting knees on floor. Slowly slide legs back. Once certain of balance, carefully push up and down.

c Front sit ups: Ready position. Lie on back with with feet together.

d Slightly bend your legs upward. Put hands behind head in clasp position, lift upper shoulders to sit up position. Twist body and shoulder to the left, touching elbow to left knee.

e Repeat sit up. Twist body and shoulder to the right, touching elbow to right knee. Repeat 20 times.

c

d

e

Back Push Ups

a

b

a Raise both legs upward. Cross them together. Pick up head and upper back 12" off the floor. Repeat 20 times. Good for abdominal.

b Lie on back, feet shoulder width apart. Bend feet upwards, placing hands by shoulders.

c Place hands and feet flat on the floor. Pick up body as high as you can by placing weight equally on feet and hands. Hold for two counts, and repeat.

d, e
Repeat as above by placing weight on head.

c

d

e

a

b

Knee Stretching

a, b, c, d

You have now completed your leg stretching. At this time, return to a standing position with feet together and place hands on the knees. Bend and straighten the knees in a small gentle movement, followed by a circular motion, three times clockwise, then counterclockwise. This loosens the knee joints. Next squat down as if going into sitting position keeping hands on the knees, then stand up, bend at waist and keep your back straight to stretch the back muscles. Shake the legs, shoom-she-ge.

c

d

Chapter 2

RUNNING
Water Log and Meditation

CHAPTER 2

- My Favorite Aerobic Exercise

If you have never explored running and wish to, I encourage you to do so after you have a doctor's permission. One must have a very good pair of shoes, with a high support for the heel area. Wear the lightest clothing for given weather conditions. Layer clothing, starting with a base of shorts, T-shirt, and a good pair of cotton socks. Running develops the thigh muscles. Start by jogging to stretch the leg muscles slowly, allowing them to adjust to the movement. Try not to pound on the feet after the first half-mile. Always run lightly, landing on the heels of the foot. Never land on the entire foot. The secret to successful running is moving the feet and legs in a circular movement as you run, stepping on the heel lightly, and pushing off with the ball of the foot and toes. This avoids heavy pounding on the entire foot and body. Pounding makes a runner's legs tire quickly and muscles tighten.

For the first few days running, you should not try to increase your speed. Continue jogging twice a week for two to three weeks for approximately one to two miles per session. This gives a new runner time to learn to adjust his breathing and increase stamina.

It is very important to keep the back upright when running. The steps must be high, legs circling in a heel-toe motion as you move forward, head up, hands positioned at shoulder level, maintaining a constant speed at all times during training.

I suggest that you begin a new running program during the spring or summer when the weather is more conducive to outdoor running. Before running, drink enough water and prepare by stretching to prevent muscle tightening.

Continue this pattern for at least a month before you begin to add distance to your running program. When adding distance, you must be prepared to acknowledge and deal with some pain, as you will be building stamina. Expect this pain and go through it. If you feel very uncomfortable, of course, stop. Once again, it is very important to maintain regular breathing and a relaxed constant pace. Increase your distance from your initial one to two miles or three after the first two weeks. Continue increasing as you wish. You could even increase to marathon distances if you are dedicated to do so!

Running develops stamina needed for tae kwon do and karate training. There are many aerobic exercises which accomplish the same goal, such as biking, swimming and so on. Another excellent exercise for developing stamina, strength and speed is jumping rope. Be sure to land on the balls of the feet and gradually increase the speed of the rope. You can progress to jumping rope with only one leg or jumping rope by hopping back and forth, left and right.

Water Log

Drink before you start running or fighting. When you sweat, I recommend one liter or (33 fluid ounces) per hour while exercising. Drinking too much water can and will lead to vomiting, seizures, and possible comas. Always drink in moderation. When you dehydrate the body, sodium is washed out, so you must make certain to drink water even if you are not thirsty. During the course of running, plain water may not be sufficient to re-supply the sodium that the body is releasing in the sweat and urine. Therefore a sports drink containing extra sodium is suggested. Women are slower runners and especially susceptible, because their bodies retain more water. Too much drink will also cause symptoms of hyponatremia (same as dehydration). The best solution is to consume salty foods to restore the body's sodium level before any strenuous exercise.

Meditation

Meditation is important for training and calming the mind. Concentration, focus and control are demanded in martial arts to achieve physical as well as spiritual fulfillment. It is the secret formula: to train the mind, to do more and beyond the physical limits of the ordinary man, to concentrate and think positively without disturbance. Be aware, allow the body and mind to act as a single unit. The energy and power should travel from the mind and control the body. Focus and literally do anything you set out to do. Meditation can be practiced standing or sitting, outdoors or indoors. Fears are overcome through meditation and desires are achieved but always in a quiet environment with eyes open or closed.

Sit on the floor and cross the legs in a comfortable position. Keep back straight. Place hands palm down on knees. Meditate as long as the mind is set. Take your time, think of nothing but peace without disturbances.

Focus to overcome fear.

Chapter 3

STANCES, KICKING, BLOCKING AND FALLS

CHAPTER 3

Stances, Kicking, Blocking and Falls

The study of Martial Art must start with a basic stance to improve balance, positions, walk, turn, block and fall. It is important to know how to coordinate the moves in different directions, front, back, side ways. For attacks and blocks, practice, the techniques and movements in class. It is important to master the split second blocks and attacks as needed. Training should involve various methods that include punches, blocks, kicking and combination workout. Students must observe and try to imitate their master carefully as he demonstrates techniques.

The physical techniques of kicking and the use of the body to deliver such force must involve conditioning, involving the whole body in combinations to develop speed, force, energy and power. Flexibility comes from constant stretching to loosen joints. Stomach muscles and ligaments can be strengthened with sit ups, push ups and weight training. In order to sustain the force of the kicks or punches, excellent balance must be maintained for successful execution and completed technique with full force and extension. Hand and leg blocks are equally important as kicking for defense to avoid injuries and help prepare the next strikes. Different techniques require different blocks, but all must be executed with force and focus. Effectiveness is equal to ability in absorbing the psysical shock generated upon striking or blocking. Falling exercises must be practiced as protection against such shock injuries.

The following examples should be practiced daily until good progress is made.

Stances - Kicking

Stances - Kicking

a Normal Stance
Place both feet facing forward, one step apart. Hold both arms slightly bent at wrist.

b Back Fighting Stance
Start same as normal stance, placing front foot forward, back foot turned out at 90 degrees so that back heel is in line with front foot. Bend knees so that 80% of weight is on back leg and 20% on front leg, keep body straight, both arms bent slightly, fist close to protect side of body, face and middle targets. This stance is the most popular and practical.

c, d Front Stance
Start with normal stance, both feet facing forward, one step apart. Slide left foot forward one and a half steps, shoulder width apart. Bend left leg and lock back leg, keep upper body straight. 75% of weight on front leg and 25% on back leg. Keep feet flat on floor.

a

b

c

d

Stances - Kicking

a Tiger Stance

Same as back fighting stance except front foot is closer to back foot 1/2 step apart, back heel up. No weight rests on ball of foot, 100% of weight on back foot.

b Taegeuk High Stance

From normal stance slide left leg forward one step from right leg, front foot facing forward and back foot facing 45° outward. Place 85% of weight on back foot. Keep back straight.

c, d Horse Back Stance

Start at normal stance. Slide left leg sideways, parallel to right leg with both knees bent outward. Distribute weight equally on legs until you feel the tension on your thighs. Keep back straight and tuck fists at hips.

a

b

c

d

Stances - Kicking

a

b

a Double Wrist Block
Hold finger tips together. Bend wrist at palm. Pick up left leg. Swing both arms across chest to the sides, wrist facing up. Lock right knee and place arms slightly bent above respective shoulder.

b Open Hand Double Low Block in Tiger Stance
From back stance strongly swing both open hands across chest palm down. Rest your left foot on ball of foot.

c Combination High and Low Blocks
Front stance shift left leg two steps to left side. Bend knee and tilt body putting more weight on left leg. Lock your right leg, toes facing front. Simultaneously crossing both arms across chest. Tilt hip forward slightly and place right arm block locked with palm facing thigh and left bent hand block by left side of face wrist palm facing left ear.

c

Front Kick

a

b

c

a Front Kick
From front stance bend right leg so knee is facing forward. Curl toes and aim ball of foot to the floor. Extend both hands side ways with fist. Look forward, eyes focused.

b
Same as above. Extend right leg forward, lock knee and aim kick to middle section. Keep toes bent and use ball of foot for strike.

c Jumping Front Kick
From back stance, pick up left leg as high as you can, touching left knee to chest, swing kicking leg forward and up while jumping in mid air. Kick with ball of foot.

d High Front Kick
Same as middle front kick. Pick up and swing kicking leg forward to face level.

d

Round House Kick

a, b

Most effectively used kick in fighting and breaking. From back stance pick up kicking leg (back leg), right foot, and bent knee. Parallel to floor, pivot left leg to the side and back while swinging right hip forward.

Snap right leg to middle section. Bend toes and use ball of foot for strikes. Drag back right leg quickly back to fighting stance. Targets are to stomach, ribs and chest.

c, d

Instep Roundhouse kick can be executed while walking, hopping, and from back stance. While shifting weight to front foot, raise back foot, snap kick toes straight to target. This kick is effective to middle and high sections. It can be used as multiple kicks.

a

b

c

d

Side Kick

a Most used in fighting and breaking. Start with back stance.

b Bring back foot right leg bent up and shift it forward. Place foot by left knee. Keep foot straight and fists by the chest. Pivot left leg side way while aiming kicking leg forward in bent position. Focus eyes on target.

c Snap right leg forward using the outer edge of the leg. Extend right hand along kicking leg and place left hand at chest area. Lock the kicking leg. Bring back right leg, placing foot by left knee returning to fighting stance. This kick is effective to knees, solar plexus, ribs, neck and face areas. It is a very powerful kick.

d Side kick face area same as above. Raise right leg out and up to face area, or neck.

a

b

c

d

Back Kick

a Start from back stance. While on the floor bend back leg slightly.

b Shift weight on front leg. Pick up back leg. Turn shoulders and body forward with eyes focused on target. Shift weight to back foot.

c, d
Snap right leg forward. Lean upper body slightly to the back. This kick is useful to the middle section. Ribs, chest, face and knees are all targets for this thrust kick. Very effective in fighting and breaking.

a

b

c

d

Walking Side Kick

a Side shifting of legs is an excellent exercise for sick kicks, low, middle and high, good for stretching and foot workout to enhance speed, balance and accuracy.

b From normal stance cross place kicking leg in front or in back of standing leg.

c Pick up kicking leg with bent knee and right hand bent with fist on top of left hand; both fists by left side of the hip.

d Snap kicking leg to middle section using outer edge of leg placing right hand along kicking leg and back hand protecting the chest.

a

b

c

d

Blocking

a, b, c
Low block

Start in normal front stance, left leg forward. Make fists with both hands. Pick up left arm across the chest positioned by right ear. Right arm should be under left arm across lower part of chest. Simultaneously snap left arm down with palm up across the chest to left thigh and right hand to right hip. This block should be practiced walking forward, backward and sideways and often changing arms is effective against kicks, grabs, low punches and to protect the groin areas.

a

b

c

High Block

a, b, c, d
High Block

Front stance, left leg forward. Make a fist with both hands. Place left arm bent at elbow cross by right hip, right hand bent at elbow up by right ear. Together and simultaneously snap left arm up, wrist up over forehead and right hand by right hip. Use a twist on the arms to add power. This block is useful for kicks, punches or weapons attack from overhead.

a

b

c

d

Outside Inside Middle Block

a

b

a, b
Outside Inside Middle Block

From back stance, pick up blocking right hand above right shoulder. Position left arm bent in front of middle section palm down. Keep both hands in fists. Swing blocking right hand forward strongly to chest with palm in, bent elbow parallel the shoulder. Twist slightly forward. Place left arm by left hip with fist palm face down. This block can be done in front stance and horse back stance. It is useful in blocking, punches, kicking and weapons.

c

Repeat same middle block for open palm middle block.

c

a   b   c

a, b, c
Inside Outside Middle Block
Back stance, right leg forward. Make fists with both hands. Put blocking right bent hand under bent left hand. With both palms down, together swing right hand out and place by right shoulder. Palm of left hand bent with wrist palm up, applying a force on right blocking hand.

d
Front Stance Double Low Block
From front stance, left leg forward. Make fists with both arms and swing cross chest down with a strong force, palms facing legs. Excellent use in forms and double strikes.

There are many ways of blocking and maneuvering different hand and leg positions. Hand blocks and kicking strikes should be practiced repeatedly with the help of a master.

d

a Double Middle Block

Back Stance. Cross hands in front of chest with palm in, arms bent.

b Place hands at shoulder height and elbows by ribs, repeat same with palms out.

c Double Hand Low Block

Back stance. Make fists with both hands. Swing blocking left arm across the chest and right arm by right rib palm down.

d Sweep blocking left arm down six inches from your thigh. Palm down, place right hand chest high palm up, and apply force to both hands.

Knife Hand Middle Block

a

Middle knife hand block starts from back stance left leg forward. Place open knife left hand by right ear and right open knife hand by hip, palm down.

b, c

Together snap both arms placing edge of left knife hand cross forward by shoulder height and right hand with palm up by solar plexus.

This middle block knife hand is used against strikes to chest, stomach, ribs, solar plexus. It is the most commonly executed knife hand and can be applied to low sections against kicks and weapons as well as high block.

a

b

a Double Hand Low Block

Front Stance, left leg forward. Make fists with both hands. Pick up arms, bend and position them by right hip. Together thrust both fists down with wrists crossed. Right on top of left positioned at groin, focus forward and repeat this block to right side. Switch legs. This double low block can be applied with open knife hand to defend grab leg strike or stick.

b Double Hand High Block

Same as double hand low block. When positioned by hip area, thrust hands forward and up, crossing wrists and fists above forehead. This block can be done with open knife hand. Effective for blocking legs and hand strikes to the face.

a Fist Low Block

As opponent strikes with middle punch, step to the outside. Block with the right arm, fist palm down, throwing striking arm off target. Same technique can be applied from inside. Low fist block is useful for blocking leg strikes.

b Double Hand High Block

When opponent strikes with a punch to the face, step to the side in front stance and simultaneously cross arms in front of chest. Block with right hand palm in and left arm palm up, supporting right elbow. This power block can be used for arm and leg strikes.

c Double Hands High Block

Repeat as double hand high block. Use both hands, palms facing each other to block.

d Double Knife Hand X Block

Thrust open knife hands down, cross wrists, to block low strike. For high punch, thrust knife hands up forward. Can be used to block low punch, low kick, and weapons.

a High Knife Hand Block
   Thrust open knife hand forward, up high to
block opponent's strike. Can be used in front or
back stance, stepping in or out of opponent's
stance.

b Leg Block
   Side kick block to the knee. This can be used
to block opponent's front kick at knee or at
instep by blocking with low side kick before
the opponent raises his kick high enough.

c, d Crescent Kick Block
   As the opponent strikes with a punch or front kick, raise the blocking leg in circular motion
and block wrist or arm with sole of the foot. This block can be used for low and high strikes.

Falling

Falling is basic and a most important practice to avoid injuries as well as to increase flexibility and good timing when facing opponents. You must know the proper way to fall when being pushed, thrown or shoved. Follow the exercises below and practice many times.

a Left Side Fall
Start with normal stance. Open left hand palm down and bend your arm with open hand in front of left shoulder. Start to fall by bending your knees.

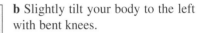

b Slightly tilt your body to the left with bent knees.

c Continue to fall by bending knees down and prepare to touch your hip with extended left arm.

c

d

c Touch left palm with the support of the left shoulder.

d Thrust both feet forward to the right and fall on the floor. Slap left palm with locked elbow. As soon as you touch the floor, raise both legs.

a Right Hand Fall
Repeat as left hand falls; right falling on right side.

b Slap right palm on the floor with support of the right shoulder, raise both legs.

a

b

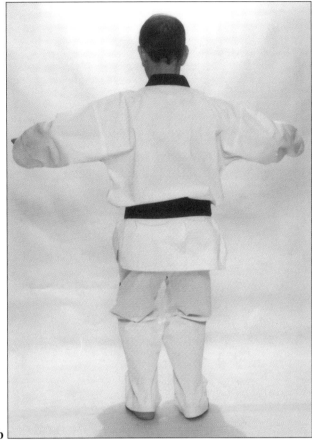

b Bend your knees to squat position.

d Slap both palms on the floor and lock elbows. With the support of the shoulders, raise both legs in the air. Keep head up!

a Falling Backwards
Start with normal stance. Extend both arms forward slightly bent, palms down.

c Continue falling. Touch the floor with your hip first while crossing both hands in front of your face.

Chapter 4

BREATHING AND YAA

Breathing

When preparing for fighting or breaking techniques, students often get emotionally and mentally tense. This affects their physical movement and leads to loss of speed, power, focus and flexibility. By breathing properly in a relaxed manner, nerves calm and you can help avoid stress. Coordination of movement with breathing will aid your flexibility. Especially in fighting when the opponent is in constant movement, you must focus your energy and apply techniques without hesitation. The body should move naturally and connect with the mind, be free of tension to allow flow, and to avoid jerky movement. The mind should be directed consciously towards reaching the target. Always take time when breathing to release tension, to slow your motion and relieve tension. Students should not hold their breath as it will cause tension that could transfer shock to muscles and cause loss of flexibility. Exhale through the mouth and inhale through the nose. Expand the diaphragm completely by moving your arms in a circular motion as you exhale. Force all air from lungs. Without any measurable pause, inhale, lifting the chest, shoulders and arms, inflating lungs to their fullest.

Yaa

Yaa is a variation of breath control. It should be loud enough to cause an opponent to hesitate and obstruct his mind. Breathing is a way to increase strength at the moment of impact. Maximum muscular contraction of the stomach area is essential. All extra oxygen must be released as you yell.

To develop the yaa, exhale all air in your lungs and diaphragm. Yell loud to better enable muscle contraction and absorption of blows.

a, b, c, d, e, f

Start from normal stance. Open your palms. Raise palms in front of chest simultaneously. Inhale through your nose keeping mouth closed. Use diaphragm only. Take in air through your nostrils, slowly raise hands overhead. Separate your arms to sides, completing inhalation when diaphragm has expanded to the maximum. While extended outwards cross chest and shoulders, begin a downward circular motion as you exhale and release without any pause all extra oxygen stored in the body.

Repeat this breathing exercise twice in between other activities.

d

e

f

Chapter 5

HANDS AND FEET STRIKING WEAPONS

CHAPTER 5

It is very important for a martial artist to know the "striking weapons" areas of the body - and the vulnerable points of the opponent. All martial artists must know the weapons that they "carry" for striking their opponent.

Conditioning the Hands

To begin conditioning the knuckles, it is recommended that a soft pad, heavily cushioned, be used initially. (It is important that students do not push themselves too hard and too fast or injury may result). The striking surface of the fist is the second and third knuckles of the hand. These knuckles may be further strengthened by knuckle push-ups, resting the body weight on the first two knuckles and completing as many push-ups as possible. This strengthens the hands, wrists and knuckles for the front punch. This is essential for effective techniques in sparring and breaking. The striking surface of the hand must be toughened to absorb pain.

I soak my hands in warm water with a small amount of dissolved rock salt to reduce swelling. Initially you may want to apply ice intermittently for twenty minutes at a time when there is no physical damage to the hand.

As you progress, and the hands toughen, harder objects may be used for punching practice, including oak boards, punching bags, even trees. Knife hand and ridge hand strikes can also be done against these objects to strengthen the sides of the hand.

All of the hand techniques used in breaking or sparring require you to condition them. As I have mentioned already, one of the best hand training conditioner exercises is push-ups, especially knuckle push-ups, performed with the weight of the body on the first two knuckles of the hand, i.e., the index and middle finger knuckles, placed approximately eight inches from the shoulders, the body held perfectly straight, not allowing the lower back and buttocks to sag. Perform the push-ups slowly at first, increasing the speed as you progress. A further strengthening exercise for the knuckles is to place your legs on a chair with the lower part of your body resting on your knuckles on the floor and do pushups in this position. This requires greater hand strength and will vastly improve strength if practiced consistently because you are lifting more weight than normal floor push-ups.

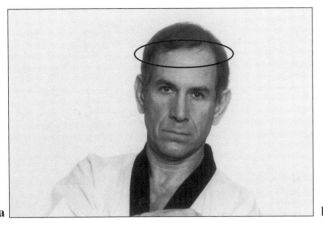

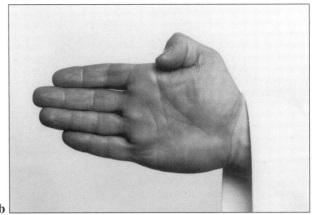

a

The Forehead can be used to strike the face and to help with throws.

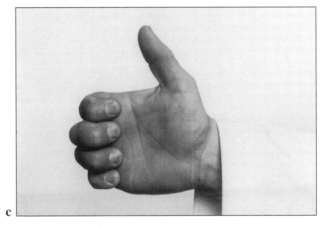

b, c, d
Fore-fist and Knuckles
The fist is the most widely used part of the body in fighting and breaking. It is very important to make a proper fist. Curl the fingers into the palm and close curl.

e, f
Place the thumb firmly over the forefinger and middle finger to prevent them from jarring lose upon contact. The closed fist is used for punching any part of the body and is effective for blocking strikes.

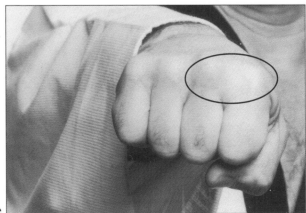

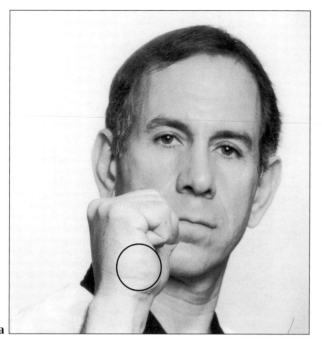

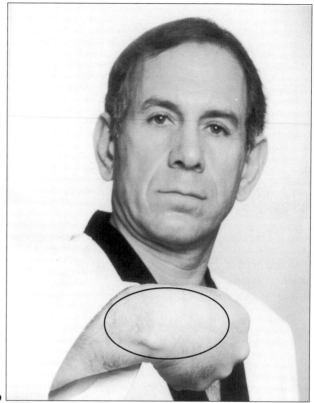

a Hammer Fist
Same as fore-fist, using the outer edge of the fist.

b, c Wrists
Extend four fingers and thumb to meet together. Bend hand inwards so that the back of the wrist is exposed forward. Use for striking a punch with snap. Upward, downward, sideways.

d Back Fist
Use the first two knuckles for strike with the wrist. Bend inward, contact with the top of the knuckles and outer part of fist. This strike is used to the face, temples and for blocking.

e Back Forearm
Lower forearm flat area. It is used to strike face, chest and throat.

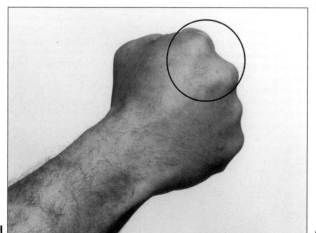

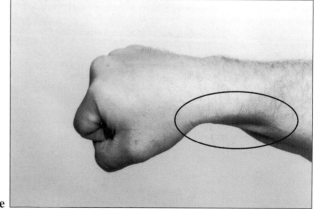

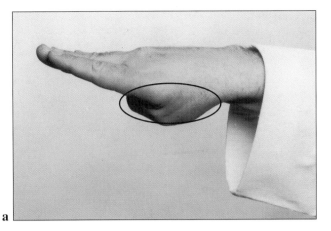

a Ridge Hand
Extend fingers but hold tightly together straight out, pull thumb in to palm, slightly bend four fingers and use the area of the first knuckle and index finger.

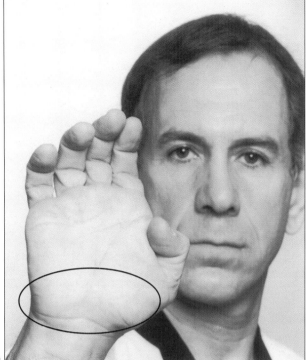

b Palm Heel
Bend your wrists backwards, curl fingers and thumb inward. Use heel of palm, snap hand for striking to the face, stomach, chin.

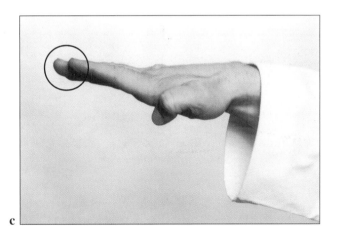

c Spear Hand
Extend fingers but hold tightly together, curl thumb against palm. Strike with the tip of fingers. Effective for throat, ribs, and solar plexus attacks.

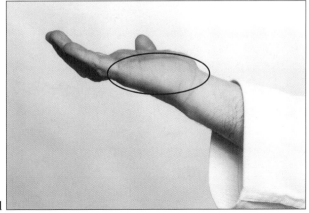

d Knife Hand
For knife hand, use the outer surface edge of the hand, extend fingers and keep hand rigid.

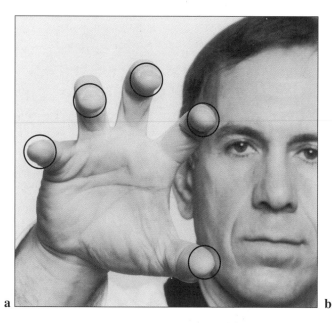

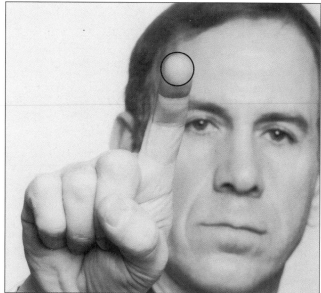

a Five Fingers
Bend slightly toward the palm using tips of fingers, striking to the face, neck and eyes. It may be used for grabbing.

b One Finger
Close all three fingers, with thumb curled over middle finger. Open first finger while creating fist with others.

c, d
Two Fingers
Extend forefinger and middle finger. Close other fingers as above.

e The Thumb
Use surface of thumb. Bend other fingers. Striking areas are the temple, throat and other parts of the body.

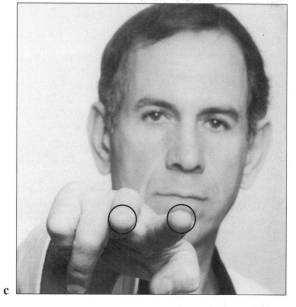

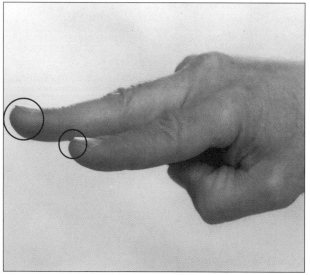

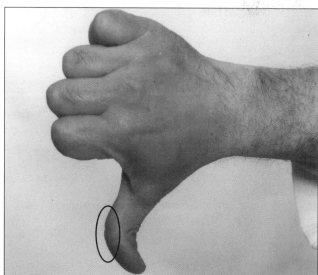

100

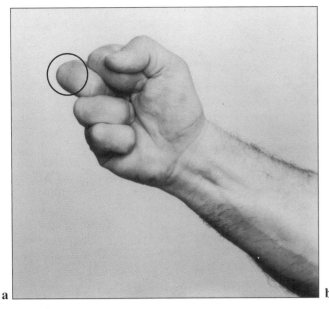

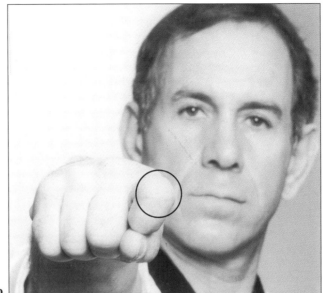

a, b One Knuckle

Make a fist and extend middle finger knuckle bent out. Use the outer part of knuckle surface, same use as forefinger knuckle.

c Two Knuckles

Bent out forefinger and middle knuckles. Clamp thumb against ridge of hand.

d Open Mouth Hand

Keep all fingers extended and thumb open. Use the curved part between the forefinger and thumb. Used mostly for choking and grabs.

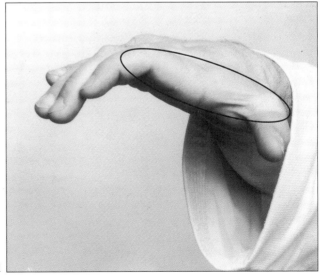

Elbows

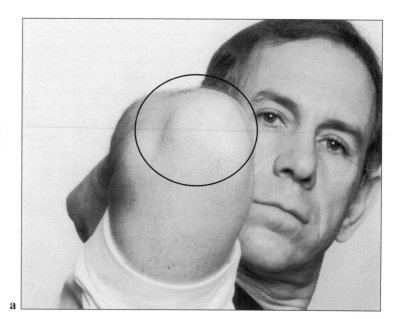

a The elbow is the joint point of the arm. Don't use the joint itself. Use only bottom, back or outer area.

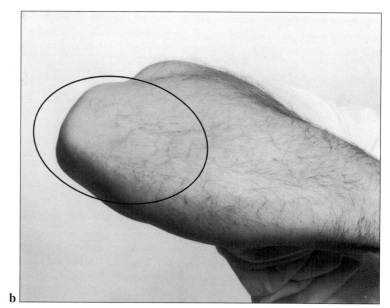

b Elbows can be directed upwards, backwards, forwards, and sideways.

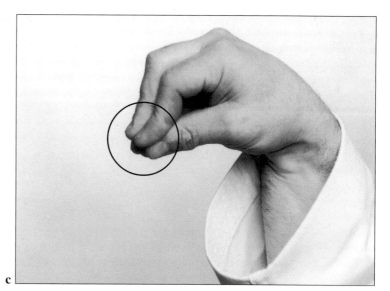

c Finger Tips:
All fingers should be together and held firmly against the thumb, finger tips bent downward.

Feet Striking Weapons

The ball of the foot is used for front kick and roundhouse kick strikes. The heel of the foot is used for heel kicks and back kicks. The side of the foot is used for side kicks, wheel kicks, crescent kicks, outwards and inwards. The instep of the foot is used effectively in front kicks and roundhouse kicks to all different parts of the body, including the head and chest attacks. The crescent kick could be used effectively using the arch of the foot for striking the knees; it could also be used effectively in a knockout and is often used by Chinese kick boxers. All of these striking body weapons may be used to attack the vital points of a fighter. A true martial artist should learn the vital parts carefully and know the danger as he attacks as some attacks could be deadly. All parts of the foot require conditioning.

Training Points

Students must use strengthening exercises to toughen leg muscles (mainly hamstrings and quadriceps of the thigh) when the foot is used as a striking object. The absorption of the blow extends through the entire leg so it must be conditioned to absorb blows and to perform kicking techniques accurately, powerfully, automatically, and without premeditation.

Most Tae Kwon Do students train in a wide stance, i.e., the horseback stance, to develop their leg muscles. The longer the time spent in this stance, the stronger the leg muscles become in preparation for kicking.

Applications in Fighting and Breaking

• Kicking techniques are divided for direct forward kicks, circular kicks and twist kicks.

• A direct kick travels in a straight line from the kicker to the target area. Examples are the front kick, side kick, and back kick. The round house kick travels in a circular motion from the outside part of the body to the inside, as does the wheel kick and the crescent kick.

• Both direct and circular kicks can be delivered in any number of ways, e.g., from one foot planted firmly on the ground to jumping in the air with the entire body to spinning 180 degrees.

• Most kicks are delivered from the back stance position with the body weight distributed so that seventy to ninety per cent of the weight is on the back leg. The front leg is pointed towards the target with the back leg turned to a forty-five to ninety degree angle to the front leg. Unlike other systems, such as in tae kwon do, most of the kicks are delivered to the middle and the upper sections of the opponent's body.

Feet Striking Weapons

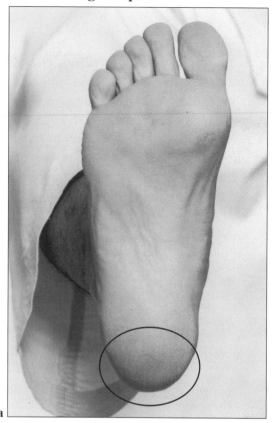

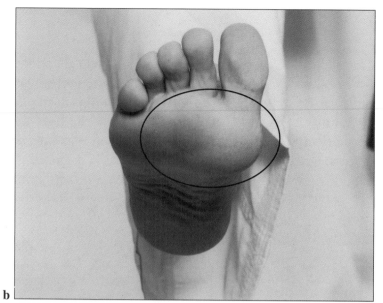

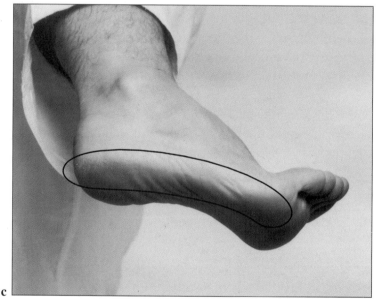

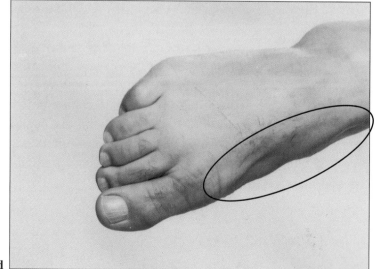

a Bottom Heel
Use the bottom part of the heel for breaking and stomping downward.

b Ball of Foot
Curl toes upward as far as you can so ball of foot projects out. This area should be conditioned as it is often used for front kicks, round house kicks and, especially, breaking.

c Knife of Foot
Use the outer edge of the foot. It is the most common striking area for side kicks, turning kicks and wheel kicks.

d Instep
Curl toes downward. Use the outer part of the foot for breaking and fighting. Effective for front kicks and roundhouse kicks, middle and face areas.

Feet Striking Weapons

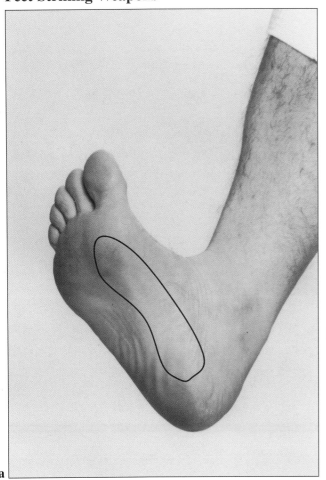

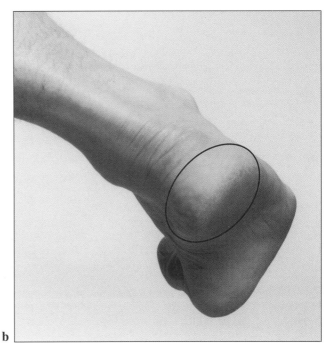

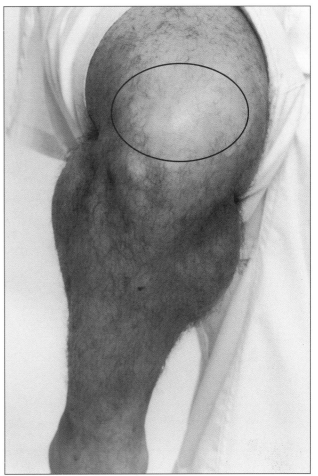

a Arc of Foot

Use the inner arch part of foot for blocking arms and leg strikes with crescent kicks.

b Back of Heel

Use the rear of heel. It may be used in different directions for hook kicks. Heel kick downward is used for breaking as well as fighting.

c Knee

Knee contact area is located approximately two inches above knee cap itself. It is used for strikes to the face, groin and body.

Chapter 6

EQUIPMENT USE

Equipment Use

The use of equipment helps to condition all parts of the body by developing strength, stretch, energy, focus, speed, endurance, coordination and most importantly stamina. It also toughens the striking surfaces of the feet, forearms and hands. The following use of equipment will help to demonstrate their use in training.

a Punching Bag

The bag is an excellent target for punching as well as kicking. It allows you to practice different ways and directions, including jumping techniques. It has the feel of a counter attack with resistance.

Wear light leather gloves, use front punches, round punches and elbows for speed, power and accuracy.

b Turning Hook Kick

c Turning Back Kick

Strike with sole of foot.

a

b

c

Equipment Use

a Back Fist/Makiwara Board
Using back of first knuckles or flat section of the fists between wrist and knuckles.

b Ridge Hand/Makiwara Board
Stand to the side, hit with flat part between thumb and forefinger, palm down.

c Hand held targets are extremely important for speed coordination and focus.

d Knife Hand/Makiwara Board
Both hands are effective for toughening striking surface and building speed.

a   b

a, b Jumping Rope
Helps to develop strength, stamina, hand & leg coordination, speed and good timing.

c Makiwara Board Spear Hand
Open palm, hold fingers together tightly. Tuck thumb by ridge of hand. Bend second finger slightly and hit makiwara board in slow motion to help strengthen with finger tips. This will strengthen finger tips.

c

a

a Knife Hand/Makiwara Board
Stand to side, strike with the outer edge of hand, palm up. Very effective in fighting and breaking strikes.

b Roundhouse Kick /Makiwara Board
With ball of foot bend your toes.

c Side Kick/Makiwara Board
Use edge of foot. Very effective as a means of toughening the edge of the foot for breaking.

d Front Kick/Makiwara Board
Ball of foot. Use both legs, strike low and high.

b

c

d

Wall Bar

Excellent for leg stretching front, side and backwards.

a Front Kick
With light hand support to maintain body balance, extra extension will be achieved on kick stretches. Good stretches are preparation for roundhouse kick, side kick, back kick.

b Leg Pull Up
Sit on the floor and grab wall bar with both hands, with most of your weight on back and shoulders. Pull up both legs, lock knees and hold for five counts. Repeat as many times as you can. Good for solar plexus.

c Jumping Flying Side Kick
Grab wall bar with both hands and jump sideways, positioning kicking leg and back leg in proper height and place.

b

a

c

Chapter 7

FAVORITE WEIGHT TRAINING

CHAPTER 7

Completing a total body weight-training regimen two times per week is essential for both health and martial arts training. I advise that you seek out a complete weight-training program from your local gym that complies with ACSM or NSCA guidelines. The regimen will include upper body pushing and pulling movements, lower body, abdominal and back movements.

My favorite weight training workouts include bench press, squats, arm curls, dumbbell rows, good-mornings and dead lifts. I execute sets of 10-12 reps at a weight at which I need to rest between sets. I wait one minute between sets. The muscles respond well to this rest period. I increase the weights I use if I can continue beyond 12 reps without a rest. I also wait at least 48 hours in between complete body weight training workouts.

First Exercise - Bench Press

Begin with very low weights, such as twenty pounds. Lie on the bench with legs straddling the side of the bench. Adjust your hands in a symmetrical position on the barbell to prepare for lifting. Exhale as you lift the bar up to an almost locked arm position and inhale as you bring the barbell down towards the chest. This exercise works the triceps, deltoids, and upper chest muscles.

For further triceps conditioning, push-ups are mandatory. Other than palm push-ups, try to execute the push-ups using the knuckles of your fists. Do 10-20 push-ups and eventually progress to 50 or more. You can also try one-hand push-ups.

Second Exercise - Dead Lifts

Adjust the weights on the barbell to your weight purposes with the guidance of a fitness professional. The dead lift begins from a standing position, feet almost double shoulder width apart, barbell resting on the floor in front of your feet. Bend your knees, reach down and lift the bar by straightening the knees, hands gripping the bar. Lift the bar first to the shoulders, then over the head locking the arms into position for a few seconds. Then, lower the bar to shoulder level, then waist level. Bend the knees and place bar back on floor. Repeat this exercise 10 times, five counts to lift, five counts over head and five counts to return starting position.

This exercise strengthens the legs, back, arms, and spine.

(Note: Between weight lifting exercises, rest for a minute.)

Third Exercise - Arm Curls

This exercise strengthens the biceps. The back and stomach muscles assist in the exercise. Face a mirror to make sure that you use just your elbow joints and not your back or shoulder joints to lift the weights. Place your feet shoulder width apart. Grasp a dumbbell with the appropriate weight in each hand. From the standing position, arms at your sides, palms holding dumbbells face forward, bend the elbows, bringing the weight towards the shoulder joint. Repeat this exercise in sets of eight to twelve reps.

This same exercise may also be done with a bar and weights adjusted to your needs. Grasp the bar with your hands in the palms out position. Curl the bar up with both arms to shoulder position, back down to resting position, to shoulder position, back to resting, for a total of eight to twelve reps.

Fourth Exercise - Spinal Flexion

Lie face down on a bench or other piece of equipment designed for this purpose. Bend forward at the waist as your balance allows and straighten the spine. Bend and straighten 10-15 times.

Other Weight Training Exercises for the Lower Body - Squats, Calf Raises

Use a Smith or similar machine to position the barbell on your shoulders behind the head. With weights adjusted on the barbell for your ability, stand with legs double shoulder width apart, feet turned out so that the knees bend over the toes. Keep the heels on the floor at all times. Grab the bar with both hands. Bend the knees slowly until the legs are at a right angle and then straighten. Remember to exhale as you straighten the knees. Do this exercise in reps of eight to twelve.

For calf raises, hold the bar as in the squatting exercise. With the legs straight, rise up to the ball of the foot and descend back to rest the heels on the ground. Do this for 15 reps. This develops the calves for round house kicks and flying kicks.

To conclude the weight training exercises and to cool the body down, stretch out. Perhaps, from a standing position with legs about two shoulder lengths apart, extend the arms and make circular motions to ease the tension on the chest, shoulders and neck.

• There are, of course, many more exercises. Those presented here are only a very few.

Bench Press

Equipment Use

Dead Lifts

Arm Pulls

Arm Curl

Section II

FIGHTING
The Ultimate Sport

**Fighting: Never provoke a fight – fighting is to be used only for survival.
If you are forced into a fight, be prepared for the consequences of your action.**

CHAPTER 1

Fighting is a very popular and explosive sport. It is challenging in that it is a game of the mind and the body. It is for survival and entertainment. Fighting for good or evil is part of our culture and appears in games, movies, posters, advertisements, television, books and elsewhere.

David fought Goliath, the warrior and opponent of the Palestinians. There was a significant difference in physical ability between the two opponents. One opponent was of average human size and the other was a giant.

Goliath may have been the favorite to win but a good fighter always uses speed, coordination, and most importantly, intelligence.

Thinking fast will help save you. David used a rope and stone, which he aimed at Goliath's head. He won the fight and proved strength does not always make the difference. Thinking always provides the better way.

Fighting is a sport which occurs in boxing, wrestling, tae kwon do, kung fu, go-ju, ju jitsu, judo and others. The fighting skills of a fighter begin with conditioning, intelligence and speed. A good fighter uses these skills to defend himself.

Good conditioning is essential to the fighter's performance. A good fighter is always in excellent shape, which helps him compensate for the differences in height and size of his opponents.

What makes a good fighter? It is the one who trains everyday in the gym or martial arts school. One who practices the basics and utilizes all his skills during workouts and attends classes conducted by a master.

One's abilities are discovered after training hard in martial arts or at the gym. Other opponents, masters, or teachers will expose the problems in fight situations.

Fighters are often conflicted about how to approach their opponent. The first thought is often about not wanting to get hurt and the second thought is about wanting to win. Wanting to win must be the key motivator in order to become a successful fighter. When the fighter decides to take charge of his opponent, then fear leaves his mind.

• A fighter must be conditioned and well trained before he gains experience in competition fights.

Training should involve various methods. It should start with thorough stretching for about ten to fifteen minutes, then upper body work for ten to twenty minutes including punches, blocks, knife hands, turning strikes, then proceed to the lower body work that will include roundhouse kicks, circle kicks, back kicks, hook kicks, spinning kicks, pressing kicks, etc.

Kicking well is critical as the legs have a much longer reach than the hands. Most non-tae kwon do opponents are not used to being attacked by a combination of kicks and punches.

Instep Kick to the face

Fighting Stance

Side Kick to chest level

124

Training combinations of hand and foot work make up a traditional workout. A good fighter should progress from the kicking workout to a combination workout. Combinations are important for fighting strategies. One utilizes kicking and punching at the same time without stopping. This creates surprise motions, which come from all directions. One must also train to block any attack that might come from the opponent.

Combination techniques help a fighter build up his speed. Speed is the key factor of an effective fighter. Speed gives the fighter an opportunity to counteract an opponent. This includes the blocking necessary to resist an attack. To build up speed a martial artist, boxer, wrestler etc, must use targets. Suitable targets include punching bags, makiwara boards, wall targets and hand-held targets. Jumping rope will help build the speed and stamina of a fighter. A punching bag will help build and develop the punch workout of the practitioner. A punching bag can be viewed as an opponent. Hit it in all different directions, from low section, middle section, and high section using kicks and punches. From this exercise one can learn the actual weak points of the body.

Turning backwards is a way of developing speed as well as good vision. A trainee does not know how to use his vision unless his speed is coordinated with the turning motion. The punching bag can help develop combinations by throwing kicking and punching techniques in different ways. Shift the legs and hands, keeping the target in front.

Of course, using the bag is not like facing an opponent, but the feeling of standing in front of the bag and hitting it with full power kicks or punches will appear to give the feeling of the bag hitting you back. That's how the punching bag gives a fighter the sense of the opponent's power.

Obviously, most people don't think that the power of an opponent is as strong as the training opponent. An opponent who has good vision and good timing will always counterattack without hesitation. If one even doubts what to do, counterattack by stepping forward with one's combinations instantly.

By using other targets such as handheld targets, a fighter can develop speed by hitting the target with both legs and hands. The punching bag is different. One needs to train with both.

When the master demonstrates his technique, the students must follow accordingly. Observe the speed, the height and the coordination of the attack. Try to imitate.

When fellow students help by holding targets for each other, ask them to change the height and angle of the targets. This will help you learn different kicking angles. Alter your speed as well. A one-dimensional fighter does not stand a chance against a multi-dimensional fighter. Also, a student must find a good qualified master who can help develop the right as well as the left side in fighting. It always appears that many martial artists try to stick to one combination that is their best.

There are many martial artists who develop many different combinations that are their best, but in a fight, sometimes a martial artist will hesitate to use many of his attacks that he has perfected in training. Why? It is a normal human error to hesitate and not think clearly. A good fighter will not have and cannot afford to have those errors. In my opinion, a good fighter should not hesitate, should not fear and doubt himself and should not step into a fighting situation if he is not in good condition and prepared. There are always surprises in a fight that are virtually impossible to avoid and they can cause

Extended High Front Kick

serious damage if one is not prepared for them. Therefore, you must prepare yourself for all surprises, for all changes in a fighting situation in your techniques.

There is always a small possibility that confusion can occur in a fight because of the different styles that the two fighters may use against one another. A good fighter must adjust himself quickly to whatever style he encounters at a particular moment in a fight as there is not that much time to do so. It does happen where you must create your own way, defending first, giving you enough time to know and work each other. Do not become excited, stay close so that you may observe your opponent's techniques for at least the first or second round, depending on how many rounds there are in the fight.

It is obvious that the more you train, the more experience you will get, but a lot of people do not think that way. They never doubt their opponent, or enemy, and they never doubt themselves. There are so many outstanding fighters that have great ability. They have discovered it, developed and worked for it. At the same time, training is a chance to observe, talk and help correct your fighting systems.

Always go back to basics when proceeding to more advanced sparring practice. Especially in free sparring, use your judgement as to the most effective techniques to apply at any given moment. You must learn continually to deal with conflicts that face you during fighting. Plan a good strategy and respond quickly to all advanced techniques while you have the opportunity in class to learn more effective kicks and blocks, as you work out with an opponent. Train yourself to quickly defend against an attack coming at you by counter attacking with blocks, punches, kicks, and take downs, continuously monitoring limited floor space and good weight distribution on both legs. Shift rapidly to defend yourself in any situation. You may take one technique and attack rapidly using a combination of two or three techniques at any given time, catching your opponent off guard. Continuously assess your knowledge, ability, speed and your opponent's favorite techniques. Then respond by focusing on his weak points to take advantage, using your most effective combinations. When using faking techniques to test your opponent's combinations, as soon as you have an open target, you must apply and execute in rapid succession more than two or three techniques simultaneously. Be always ready to defend your opponent's attack with blocking, sweeping, dodging or throws. Avoid grabbing your opponent to eliminate set up counter attacks. Continue with rapid techniques that can land into the target.

Double Front Kicks to the chest

Turning Back Kick to rib section

Chapter 2

FREE SPARRING

CHAPTER 2

It all starts when a student learns the basic elemental techniques: the stances, kicks, punches, blocks and most important, maneuvering. All martial arts beginners obtain knowledge and instruction on how to use the body creatively for free sparing. Tae kwon do starts with three step sparring where the students face each other; one being the attacker and the other defender. The attacker will execute a low block in a front stance as he gets the signal to deliver a high punch. The defender will step back with a high block to block the attacker's high punch. He steps back three times, blocking three strikes. At the end of the third block the defender should find a clear opening and strike back with a series of techniques to stop the attacker's charge. The three step sparring sets are pre-arranged punches, blocks, kicks, etc. to give the student the basics of how to do without the worry of thinking what to do. The idea is to make it easy for the student to move along with practice. It teaches him how to execute effectively with good reflexes, effective blocking movements and confidence.

The progress continues to two step sparring, the same as three step sparring but shorter in time and steps. After the two and three step sparring are mastered perfectly, the student moves on to one step sparring. First we start with pre-arranged set with basic techniques for beginners, progressing to intermediate, then advanced. One student will execute only one technique at a time against his opponent. This leaves less time to think, so the counter attack must be quick and mastered until perfectly executed. Here the student will start to perfect timing to strike with focus and coordination. Then techniques should flow, incorporating all the basic fundamental stages, including determination, speed, creativity, power, accuracy, distance and discipline.

By now the student is ready to move on to free one step sparring, make up where he or she will apply all of the basic and prearranged techniques, with the option of adding more advanced punching, kicking, blocking, take downs, jumping, sweeping, grabbing techniques, speed and focus. Style and flair are important to show experience and ability to complete sequences, flows, and required movements. This develops good reflexes, confidence, balance, endurance and good coordination. By now the students facing each other become good partners and the two develop a dynamic pattern of pre-arranged sparing utilizing good movements and quick response to any situation.

The next stage of the free sparring is where two students face each other for back and forth sparring. Eye contact is critical for observing your opponent from top to bottom, telling you what your opponent is about to do. The eyes should focus at shoulder area in order to view the entire body, as sparring back and forth the students will use and execute fast kicks and punches to cover distance. As both partners are in motion, it is important to accurately judge distance and determine clear target openings before the attack. Back and forth sparring gives the opportunity to a student to begin this rapid stage of fighting.

The final important stage of free sparring is for students to work on their personal innovations and creativity. When the two student partners face each other in the gym or school one should not become excited. Connect the mind with the body, use good judgement. Study your opponent by maneuvering around him. Start with slow thrust movements to allow yourself time to study his reflex in the counter attack. As you progress with free sparring let your partner attack, giving you the opportunity to practice your defense techniques of blocking, evading, dodging and striking at your own discretion with proper timing to the target for the score. Judge your distance, use speed to avoid being grabbed and defeated by your partner. Always when feigning an attack follow through with a series of effectively timed tech-

High Flying Side Kicks

niques. Otherwise you will be open to counterattack and possibly set up for devastating blows. Always focus your attack with good distance, speed, power, precision and timing. Keep your rhythm utilizing different techniques. Stay calm and allow your motions and movements to flow without hesitation. You must maintain your physical strength and stamina by continuously training. The longer the fight, the more stamina needed. Keep your spirit high and pay attention to small details during the fight. Try to take control of the opponent by continuously moving, while surprising him with kicks and fast hand techniques, causing him to lose balance. At this point your purpose is to end the fight with multiple techniques in fast action and a strong yaa to deliver the final blow until the master or referee or the partner stops the fight, and you are declared the winner. You may apply these strategic ideas and experience to any situation and to any fight whether the fight takes place in a school, a gym, or in a championship. The following examples of one step sparring should be practiced to increase your knowledge and experience. Satisfaction and wisdom are on going rewards, be it tae kwon do or life.

The following examples are one step makeup

Side Kick

Counterattack with Front Hook Kick

a, b
Opponent gets ready to grab defender at the same time defender executes a fake right leg side kick to middle section.

c
Immediately defender with the same right leg while still in mid air executes front hook kick to strike opposite side of face. This technique is good to use in free sparring as effective techniques.

Double Cross Blocks and Front Instep Kick Counterattack

a

a Defender uses double cross high blocks to block opponent's punch.

b

b Defender uses a circular motion inward, grabs opponent's wrist with right hand and applies pressure on opponent's elbow with left palm.

c

c Defender pulls opponent's hand forward and kicks opponent's face with front instep kick.

Combination of Roundhouse Kick and Turning Back Hook Kick

a Defender and opponent face each other in ready stance.

b Opponent strikes defender with high punch. Immediately defender counterattacks with right leg instep roundhouse kick to opponent's upper chest area.

c Defender blocks opponent's right hand, pushes it upward placing right leg behind opponent's front leg, starts turning backward while lifting leg to striking position.

d Keep eyes open, turn quickly with good balance striking opponent's face with turning back hook kick.

136

Take Down with Counter Attack

a Defender blocks opponent's high punch with high knife hand block.

b Wrap left hand around opponent's wrist. Simultaneously take one step forward, place right leg behind opponent's front leg and strike opponent's neck with open knife hand. After strike, quickly wrap right hand around back of opponent's neck.

c Take down opponent with a hip twist motion backward until opponent takes the fall on the floor.

d At this point continue with great speed same twist motion until opponent is off the floor and falling on his left side.

e Keep grabbing opponent's right hand while executing a side kick or a heel strike to opponent's ribs.

a

b

c

d

e

137

Front Hook Kick Block and Counterattack to Face Level

a Defender and opponent at ready stance.

a

b Opponent executes a middle punch. Defender takes one step sideway with left leg, immediately executes front wheel kick with right leg blocking opponent's right hand middle punch.

b

c Defender with same blocking leg executes front hook strike to opponent's face.

c

Middle Block Punch, Combined with Turning Back Kick

a Both defender and opponent face each other in ready stance.

b Opponent starts with front stance low block.

c Opponent strikes defender with high reverse front punch. Defender takes one step forward with right leg, blocks opponent's punch with middle right hand block, stays in back stance.

d Grab opponent's right hand with left hand. Execute front punch at opponent's face with right hand.

e Simultaneously release grabbing hand. Execute turning back kick with left leg at opponent's chest.

a

b

c

d

e

Block and Counterattack with Side Kicks

a Opponent and defender face each other in ready stance.

b Opponent strikes defender with a punch to face area. Defender takes one step forward into back stance, blocks opponent striking punch with right hand middle block.

c Defender shifts front leg back, immediately continues with middle side kick to chest area.

d Quickly bring back striking left leg; use it for a snap side kick to face area.

Take Down Two Opponents

a

a Focus on distance, keep an eye on opponents.

b

b When opponents grab wrists, take one step forward with left leg into a front stance.

c

c Defender starts to swing arms backward; stay focused on opponents.

d Defender raises hands up; start circular motion up and backward above shoulders.

a

e With quick action, swing arms backward, bend forward and grab opponents' back of legs; continue this motion forward until opponents drop backward.

b

f Keep pulling opponents' legs upward to complete take down.

c

Chapter 3

WHAT A MARTIAL ARTIST SHOULD OBSERVE
Before, During and after a Fight

CHAPTER 3

Fighting qualifications – A martial artist, a boxer, a student of any contact sport must be prepared for the moment of attack. Before the fight begins, the fighter must have full control of the mind and developed theory meditation exercises. One must look directly into the eyes of the opponent in order to observe fear and steady oneself for the attack. The mind must be able to move without hesitation. Once the referee steps into the ring, or the fighting space, the fighter should be prepared to face his opponent mentally, morally, and physically. At the presentation, a fighter must stay calm, obey the rules and follow the directions of the judge because one slight mistake by not listening to the rules, or becoming overexcited, will result in a loss.

The moment when the referee enters the ring, a fighter must have full confidence, be in the ready fighting stance with full balance and coordination, and with power of concentration focused on his opponent. The fighter should be prepared for whatever the opponent may throw at him. Hesitation will result in losing valuable ground and that should not be the intention of a good fighter.

Firmly face the opponent. Focus by looking into his eyes and watching his body at all times. Concentrate on the shoulders. Look for any motion there first. Give yourself a chance to circle around the ring during those few moments. Make sure you throw attacking body motions, but not in full force, just enough to test your opponent. Whether it will be a kick or punch, one of the attacks will cause your opponent to respond.

At this point you should become familiar with your opponent's speed and force. You may predict that a fighter will use a shoulder motion to distract your focus. Respond anyway. Responding gives you clear appearance of self-confidence. This response might even be a successful attack, as maybe your opponent is slow to react.

You must rely solely on the technique and coordination from your practice session, on the fighting combinations you have stored in your mind. After the first few minutes of a fight, you will know what to expect from your opponent, whether good or bad. If your opponent is stronger than you, you must focus on your speed. If the opponent is weaker than you, you must focus on your strength, take aim at the target, to hurt, but not to kill.

Attack with kindness. Show your opponent a full motion score and move on. At times the opponent could be very aggressive, like a killing machine facing you. What should you do at that point? You must learn the weaknesses of the opponent by throwing combinations, one after the other. By feeling the reaction of your opponent, you must find the way to enter into a full attack at the right moment to score, be it a reverse punch, back kick, roundhouse, or initially, the mind.

The mind game in a fight is very important. Many fighters will test each other using mind games. For example, one fighter can laugh at the other fighter by intimidating him with unexpected moves.

A fighter should try not to fall into this trap. That's where mistakes occur. Retreat immediately, allow the opponent to charge, and give yourself a chance to gather up your thoughts. Follow-up with your attack. Remember, one combination does not always make a win. A follow-up combination will make it a win.

Your attacks may always seem perfectly executed, but a student must also judge his opponent's executions as well. Respect the opponent's execution and experience. This will help make you a winner. Quickness in following up on your attacks, the quickness of your response to your opponent's attack, is important. Look at the open target, execute and winning your point without hesitation.

There is always a chance your opponent may surprise you with an unexpected attack. Your mind may not be focused properly because of the general excitement of the fight. But take chances anyway because you will lose by not trying. You never know what your opponent's weaknesses are. The opponent might throw wild techniques without a real plan, but you must have a back-up plan at all times. That's what can save a good fighter. Use your intelligence, make it work profitably, accurately, judge yourself for excellence.

Of course, the referee looks carefully at all that is going on in the ring during the fight. At times, though, the referee does not see clearly because of the speed at which all the techniques are executed. But a fighter must stay calm, make his point, step back, follow instruction and wait for the call- whether it is a good or a bad one. If it is a bad one, stay calm and hope the next call will be a better one. Not getting excited is very helpful. Remember your meditation and the hard work that you went through. That's how control factors in. Minimize your mistakes.

Any attack towards your opponent must be accurate. Attacks must be with full combinations of double kicks, triple kicks, double punches, combinations of back kicks, hook kicks, spinning kicks, front kicks, roundhouse kicks, back fists, knife hands, front punches, etc. That's where speed and coordination of body motion come into play. It is obviously very important to use your reflexes. This is another subject we must learn.

Reflex is the result of the mind controlling the body, sending orders to the foot and the hand. The body moves instantly without hesitation following an attack.

Reflex is life saving. It will always help to develop your reflexes by training in a gym against a fellow student who understands your thinking and combinations of the fighting methods you use. This will allow you to develop better techniques. In a fight, expect the unexpected.

No one is completely prepared but it's good to have that as a goal. Take appropriate chances, even if it will result in the loss of the fight. That's where the positive works together with the negative. Not everyday is a good day for a fighter, but one can try to fight well. One must always have a positive attitude.

Fantasy does play a big part in all of us, but at the same time we must not forget reality. So in a fight, everything is possible. At one particular moment a good fighter might have so much confidence that he is leading in the fight, but it might turn out in reality that he is really distracted.

You must stay in control of your mind and body with its motions. This will allow you to go on for the win. In my early years, in the fight arenas, I did not care who I faced, whether big, small, tall, slight, giant, or superman. It did not matter. For fighting preparation, I always remembered that I knew I would always do my best.

Never think less of yourself. Never be discouraged because you get punched or kicked in the first moments of a fight. As a matter of fact, you must be aware that you will not always be the best, but you must always try your best. Always start with rule number one: respect your opponent's thinking.

The perfect fighting sequence is the one that has speed, coordination, and reflex. The fighter with control of the mind and the body is always the winner. The one who has the most massive body, attacks brutally, or has a negative attitude will always be the loser.

I always felt that in a fight if I could get the crowd on my side after the first round or two, I would win because of the positiveness that comes from the attitude of the crowd. When spectators yell, "Go" or chant your name, it is very motivating. This agitates opponents. They sometimes lose confidence. If this happens, you take advantage by pushing forward and executing your best techniques. Again, keep a positive attitude. Watch out for the fear in your mind. Move towards being the best, aim at nothing less. Try to be the winner. The excitement is to have the audience on your side. It exhilarates you and compliments your abilities. Also, the more fighting that a student is involved in, the more experience gained and the more courage the student develops.

Fighters must use their mind, body, spirit and faith to promote themselves and be the best at what they choose to be. Always push forward to do what you must do. Nobody can stop the mind and the spirit. Dreams are there to achieve and promote you. Dreams educate. Dreams should not have stop signs. A fighter can translate his best moments into achieving his best at life. Most legendary fighters have sharp minds, reflecting on life differently than the average person. Good fighters can be special leaders.

Good fighting skills give us the fortitude to continue and push us to pursue our dreams. So look forward to the next challenge. Learn to take chances in life for your ultimate fighting and bring out the best in yourself.

All decisions may not always be positive. Some fighters get out of control by doing wild things, without considering the well-being of their opponent. They use unexpected techniques that place them in a bad light. A good martial arts fighter should have a sense of sportsmanship, thinking positively of the safety of others. Therefore, if a fighter obeys the rules and regulations of the referee and the ruling organizations and stops at the moment of a call, it demonstrates good character. This is what the martial arts philosophy is all about. The brutal part of a fighter should not be tolerated.

Full contact fighting has always existed in the Far Eastern countries like China and Japan. Israel has the Krav Maga, which is mostly an exercise used by the military, with no limits. Now, there is the ultimate fighting in which the fighter faces an opponent for unlimited rounds using all techniques until one fighter wins. They are permitted to go all the way with their attacks. They are allowed to do whatever is necessary to win. This fighter faces the ultimate challenge. There are no rules to obey.

These fights use a lot of mind control techniques to create confusion. One tries to create an air of uncertainty in the opponent, causing him to lose focus. The fighter, attempting to cause confusion, shifts position and uses speed. Good eye contact counteracts this type of fighter's strategy.

Spectators react to these situations. We all remember these special movements in a good fighter. Spectators encourage good fighters to show off special elements and attacks, such as back kicks, wheel kicks, hook kicks, etc. Techniques that are not often seen can appear as surprise weapons. Using low turning hook kicks for a take down will bring cheers from the crowd. At this moment of the fight, fighters should bring out the best of themselves. Winners are creative.

Pressure is relieved with patience and control. If the fighter loses control, he can become confused, signaling weakness. Cheering and yelling can confuse the opponent. The opponent will sense if you are in full control. You should use the crowd to your benefit. Encouragement brings out the best in a fighter. Of course, you should not lose focus during these moments. Opponents will sometimes reverse the crowd to their favor.

One other point- defense is very important. Fighters with a lack of good defensive techniques will lose the fight. Opponents will take advantage of your open targets and attack without obstruction and win.

Good fighters should invest more time for training to improve their techniques. A fighter must study strategy as well. Fighting should build confidence and help develop unlimited ways to fight. Welcome the big surprises and deal with them with pride. This preparedness will bring you a lifetime of resources and memories. The more a fighter competes and fights opponents with different styles and seeks that special challenge, the more his skills improve.

Fighting Techniques

a

a Knife Hand Block
As opponent throws a punch to your face, quickly step to the side, block arm at elbow with knife hand block.

b Knife Hand Strike
Immediately thrust same knife block to side of opponent's neck with knife hand palm down.

b

c Jumping Turning Kick
To perfect turning back jumping kicks or hook kicks, you must use a target to adjust height, extension and work on speed, coordination, timing and balance.

d Jumping Turning Kick
When you throw two or three techniques and the opponent is off balance, counter attack with a jumping turning crescent kick, spinning backwards to the left in mid air. Use back foot from back stance, lift leg upward to strike the face.

c

d

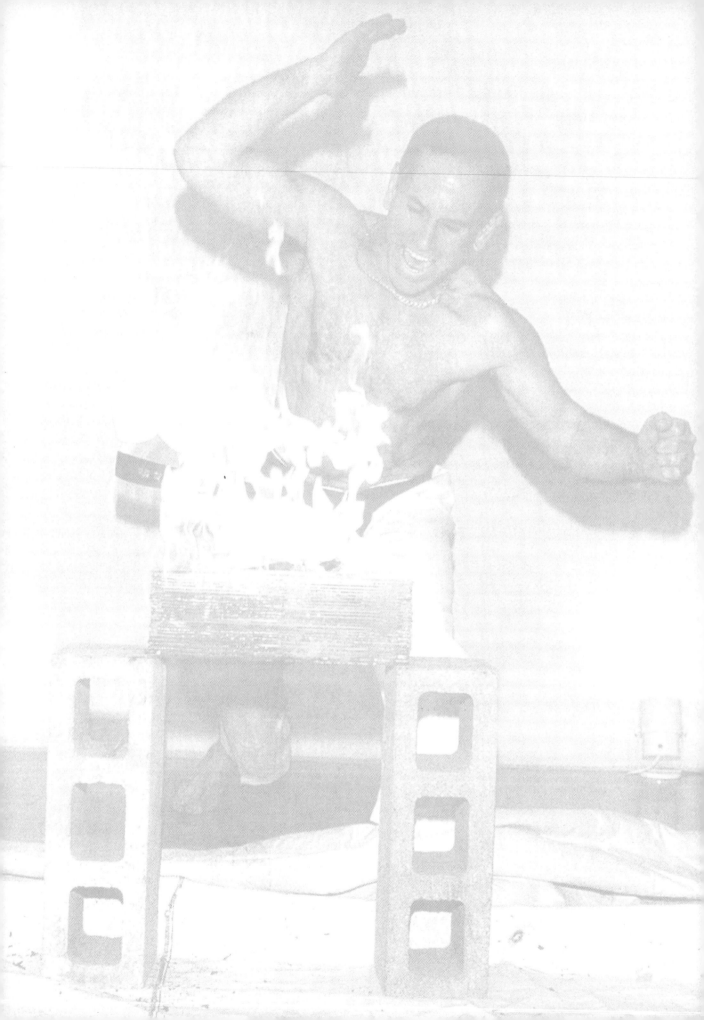

Chapter 4

MY RECOMMENDATIONS TO WIN

CHAPTER 4

First, a trainee or a student must always keep working on the basics to prepare himself physically. Warm-up, stretch and follow the traditional workout system of kicking and punching with targets. Repetitive practice of techniques is very important. It helps to build up the power in your system so you can depend on it.

Second, the experience comes not only from the gym where you face your fellow students as opponents, but from participating in as many competitions as possible. This gives you the chance to use your techniques against a variety of styles. Fighting different opponents with different backgrounds and experiences is always the most challenging part of the fight. But one must remember that by taking those chances one eliminates fear and gets the chance to prepare oneself for the most challenging moments of the fight.

Third, a fighter must not hesitate at any moment to take chances. Everything in a fight is a gamble. Anything is possible- the possibility exists to win or be defeated. A good fighter must always be prepared mentally, spiritually and physically.

The mental part is meditation, done before a fight. Relax before a fight. Do not over-excite yourself as this weakens the body's nervous system.

Meditation is a key habit in the philosophy of martial arts. Many students and instructors practice and study meditation techniques to strengthen their minds. In this way, one understands himself as an aggressor and will incorporate this into his fighting program and training. Developing self-understanding and confidence in fighting avoids injury and eliminates the fear within.

Fear and lack of self-confidence will make the fighter incapable of winning. That's why meditation is a very important part of training for the martial artist. One must empty the mind of all outside thoughts. One must pay full attention to the fight moment. This is all that matters. In the mind of the martial artist, the practitioner must use all inner strength and power to avoid distractions.

When a fighter is engaged in a fight, a total calm and relaxation must take over. You must be able to control your thoughts. You must be able to discipline your skills. At the same time, you must train your mind to see the possible self-defense that will mean victory. Think positively and be ready to take as well as to give.

Meditation strips your mind of wandering. If you use your mind properly, focusing totally on the object and every action that is coming toward you, it will establish a harmony between yourself and the bout.

Meditation will strive to free the mind of all unnecessary thoughts and ideas. One must be honest and straightforward in the examination of himself. It always seems that hearing and listening with full sincerity will give you good judgment. This judgment could be the deciding factor between life and death.

The mind empty of unnecessary thought allows us to be spontaneous with our techniques. This means that at the moment of the attack, you will be focused on your particular course of action. This will allow you to attack with the same experience level as reflected in your training. Those moments that we take to meditate allow us to have a positive attitude to face day to day training routines and to perform at our best physically abilities.

The training methods in the philosophy of martial arts are very demanding and must be pursued with complete involvement. Any challenge that presents itself must be faced with calmness. Watch and respond to your opponent. The mind, the body, and the soul must be united in concert at any moment during the match. You are the best judge of your skills and ability.

The person and the art are unified; the art does not exist without the individual. The spiritual part of meditation depends on the individual, on his belief, his faith, and his attitude.

While meditating, focus solely on the subject selected to give a sense of calm. Remove all evil from the mind. The condition of the mind and the state of the being is vital. Spiritual and mental harmony should be nurtured to develop the skills of the mind and the body so that nothing can destroy the sense of self and self-worth.

A fighter must be able to face unexpected confrontation. However, a fighter must be kind and understanding to others. One must understand that people are similar to one another. This will enable one to help oneself as well as others. Meditation will help create this understanding.

Notes

When you learn to defeat the opponent's fear, he will defeat himself.

An experienced fighter must adjust himself for a successful win.

If you learn to be fluid, you will be unbeatable.

Jumping Turning Back Kick

Execution of Side Kick to the face

Chapter 5

VITAL POINTS

CHAPTER 5

Practical Advice for the Non-Competitive Fight

The vulnerable points of the human body are various and plentiful. Here is a partial list: skull, bridge of nose, eyes, below the nose, jaw, lower lip, tip of the chin, clavicle, solar plexus, groin, instep, shin, abdomen, floating ribs, ribs, armpit, windpipe, throat, neck, elbow joint, ears, temple, wrist, back, kidneys, Achilles' tendon and so on! You see my point.

Overall martial artists should view these points as targets insofar as they are worth the risk of attack. Not all of these vital points are allowed in championships and most martial arts organizations have rules and regulations for all to follow. A real fight is a different story.

Vital Points

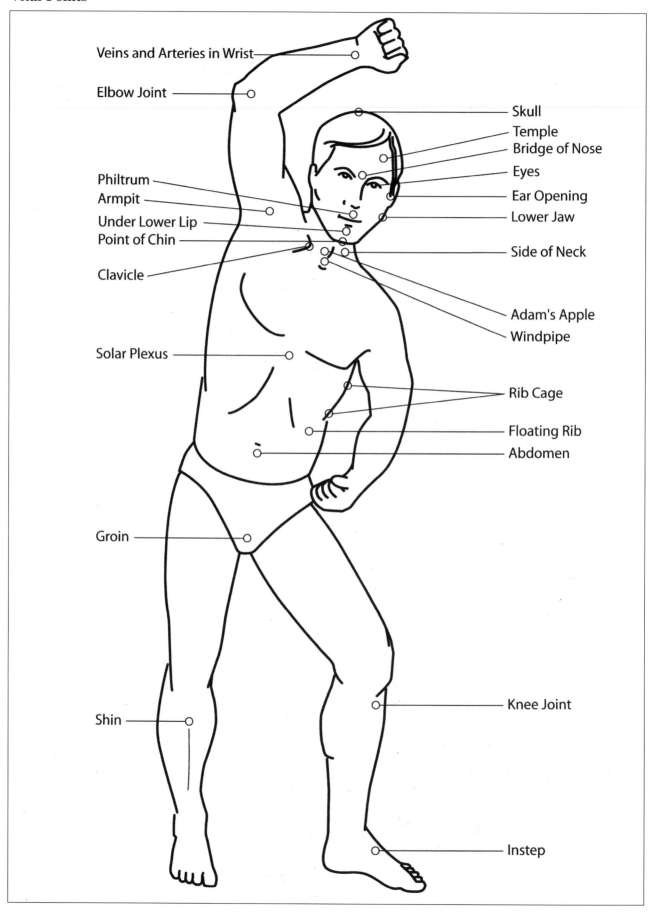

Veins and Arteries in Wrist

Elbow Joint

Philtrum
Armpit
Under Lower Lip
Point of Chin

Clavicle

Solar Plexus

Groin

Shin

Skull
Temple
Bridge of Nose
Eyes
Ear Opening
Lower Jaw

Side of Neck

Adam's Apple
Windpipe

Rib Cage

Floating Rib
Abdomen

Knee Joint

Instep

Vital Points

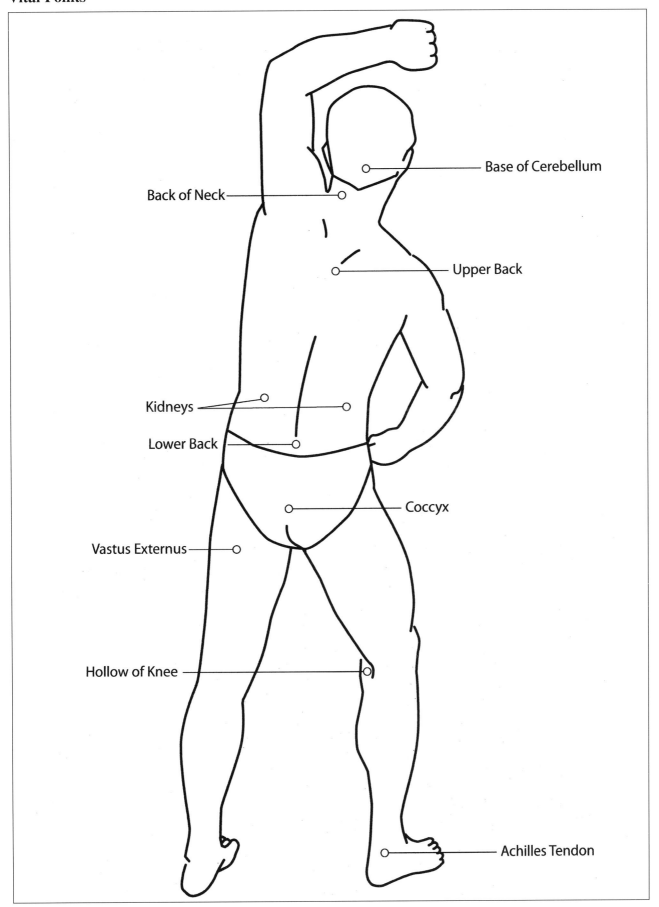

Base of Cerebellum

Back of Neck

Upper Back

Kidneys

Lower Back

Coccyx

Vastus Externus

Hollow of Knee

Achilles Tendon

Chapter 6

POINT SYSTEM
In Competitive Fighting

CHAPTER 6

One of the most common styles in championship fighting is Kumite. Two fighters face each other. It takes considerate ability to score over the constant referee's calls. The fighters face challenges when the opponent charges. One must look for the open target to score points.

There are four judges, one in each corner. The referee is in the center monitoring the fight. A call can come from any of the judges if they see a point. The majority of judges must see the point for it to count. Fighters must show the point cleanly, aiming at a clear and open target point on the opponent. That way the judge will clearly see the point.

Legal target areas are the chest, stomach area, and ribs. Sometimes they allow kicks to the head, which might even score double points from certain organizations, but none allows a punch to the face. Most tae kwon do styles do not allow punches to the face. Take-downs via a follow-up technique before the opponent hits the floor, such as a knife hand, punch, or kick are allowed in the scoring system.

Roundhouse, front, hook, wheel, swivel, and twist kicks are allowed techniques. Spear hand techniques are not allowed. Any contact to the face with an open finger technique is not allowed.

In point system, each round is two minutes with a rest period of one minute between rounds. Championships are three rounds. This is the most common rule. Some have sudden death where two opponents with an equal score are allowed to continue to the next decisive point.

The number of actual rounds varies due to circumstances. No blood is allowed in the point system. Fighters can be disqualified for this.

In the point system both fighters have many chances to concentrate and score. Often the clock is stopped due to referee calls on points scored by a judge.

The point system is safer than otherwise, due to the control of the judges and referees. The one who scores the most points, within the rounds allowed, is the winner. If both fighters have scored an equal amount of points there will be a sudden death of thirty seconds to one minute of extra time to score a winning point. The one who scores first will be the winner.

What makes the point system interesting is that both fighters must score with clean techniques to give the judges time to call the point and, given the breaks between rounds, both have time to reflect on their mistakes and correct them before the start of the next round. Because there is limited contact this makes fighting easier and safer than otherwise. Fighters have the opportunity to counterattack without fear. Of course, rules and regulations vary according to the different organizations sponsoring the championship.

In my opinion, based on experience, a fighter has less of a chance to be at his best within the point system. Fighting on the point system is more of a sport than a fight in the traditional sense of the term. With the strict rules, a fighter cannot explode freely in the point system. These restrictions limit the fighter's ability to bring out the best. I prefer freestyle systems like boxing where a fighter attacks with a two to three minute time limit. Judging occurs at the end of each round. The scorekeeper passes on the scorecards from the referee and accumulates points as the fight continues throughout the rounds. By the end of three or more rounds, the fighter with the most points is declared the winner.

Survival is life's success story. Fight for your position within the limits each system allows, inside the ring or elsewhere, but respect the life of others.

To conclude this chapter on fighting and fighting systems, I would like to emphasize that fighting rules and regulations are important. Winning depends on individual thinking and hard work. It is an uphill battle to win and develop ultimate fighting techniques. The feel of a fight is difficult to describe.

I always suggest training in the gym as many days a week as possible but not to over-train. Follow your master's advice on this. You must train with a good master; it brings out the best in a fighter. Do not hesitate to take advice from better fighters - champions with substantial experience.

The best fighters are not the ones who brag about their fighting skills in class. A true fighter expresses himself in a respectful way and leads other students. The challenge of fighting in the ring should benefit the student.

Section III

THE SCIENCE OF DEVELOPING POWER

Philosophy: The science of the mind.

CHAPTER 1

THE SCIENCE OF USING ENERGY, SPEED AND FORCE TO DEVELOP POWER

It is very important for a martial artist to know what is behind the development of key issues in the martial arts, using your basic striking weapon to the vital points of your opponents. All martial artists must know the weapons they can use to strike. We will start by using the head, continuing with the hands, legs, knees and the entire body. The head may be used to strike with the forehead and the sides of the forehead. The shoulders may be used for pushing and throwing the opponent from close contact.

First the arm. When using the fists, always lock your index knuckle with the four fingers and create a tight fist for the strike. That will allow you to use it for front punch strikes. The back fist uses the first two knuckles for striking, twisting the wrist slightly and using the back point of your fist finger knuckles. The front punch will be used straight forward, sideways, roundways, upwards, downwards. Opening your hands and tightening your fingers allows you to use the open hands as vertical spear hands, using the first three fingers for the strike. The spear hand may be used to strike horizontally, vertically, down and upwards.

Hand in open position is used for reach hand, utilizing the surface between the thumb and fourth finger. As we close our fingers halfway, we could use the two-knuckle fists, which are the first two knuckles of the hand. Then we have the four-knuckle fist, the four knuckles of the fingers. The thumb-knuckle is the thumb-knuckle as you bend it along the reach hand. As you created the same type of fists you could use the first four fingers and the middle finger that is the knuckle of the second finger.

Hammer fist is often used as a successful attack by many martial artists. This is often used for knock out, as well as breaking and self-defense. The hammer fist is the most powerful downward strike. The striking surface is the edge of the fist.

One finger attack uses the first finger, two finger attacks use the first two fingers. Open fingers in a tight knife hand utilizing the outer edge of the palm may be used striking outwards or inwards. Opening the hands in a vertical knife hand may be used for striking downwards. The palm heel is the bottom part of the open hand between the wrist and the base of the fingers. It may be used for attacks at face level, chest and other areas. A back fist attack is as effective as a front punch. Bare-hand is the whole open inside of the hand. Weeping hands could be the fingers of first finger and thumb. Back forearm uses the flat surface of the lower arm: the front forearm the inner surface of the forearm. The elbow attack is very common in martial arts for knockouts only especially used in breaking and demonstrations. The striking surface is the bottom edge of the lower forearm. This attack may be downward, upwards, sideways, front.

Next the feet. The ball of the foot is the striking surface used mostly for front and roundhouse kick strikes. The heel of the foot is used mostly for heel and back kicks. The side of the foot is used mainly in sidekicks, wheel kicks, crescent kicks, both outwards and inwards. The instep of the foot is used effectively in front, and roundhouse kicks, to all parts of the body, but especially to he head as well as chest. The crescent kick may utilize the arch of the foot for striking the knees and may also be used as a knockout or the block. This particular kick is often used by Chinese kick boxers. All of these striking body weapons may be used to attack any vital point of a fighter. A true martial artists learns the vital parts carefully and knows the dangers associated with each, including the fact that any vital part may be deadly.

The vital points of the human body begin at the head. The skull (top of the head), bridge of nose, between the eyes, the eyes, left and right, the philtrum, the part below the nose, the jaw, the lower lip, the point of chin, which is the front of the jaw, the clavicle which is the center point between the upper chest. We continue to the solar plexus, which is the center point of between the upper chest, the groin, instep, the shins, knees (right and left), abdominal, floating ribs, right and left in the lower part of the ribs in the most soft targets, the rib cage, armpit, wind pipe, Adam's apple, side of the neck, elbow joint, ears, temple veins and the arteries in the wrist, base of clavicle, back of the neck, upper back, kidneys, left and right, lower part of the spine Vastus externus, back of the knees, and the Achilles tendon.

Not all these points are allowed to be attacked in championships. Most martial artists organizations have rules and regulations for all to follow. Attacks are not allowed below the hip or to the lower parts of the body points, as well as not allowing attacks to a fighter's back.

From my experience and education in martial arts, the only commonly allowed areas are to the chest, ribs and abdominal solar plexus areas. Kicking is also allowed to these common areas. It is always recommended to the fighter to use both hands to protect his forehead, as well as chest and the open solar plexus along with any part of the legs. Blocking is allowed, and will be discussed next - how to develop the **energy** and **speed** to develop **force** and **power**.

Energy is needed to develop force and create power to make it work. It is common to use energy to push a car or an object. A common occurrence is when a martial artist is in a position too close to the opponent who is charging. There he needs energy and force to push his opponent and continue with the fight hopefully to a win. The ability to focus energy and to create force is very important. It is hard work.

The force is considered to be the main magnitude of the direct connection between the heat of the energy, but with no direction. The characteristics of the direction and the magnitude can be drawn as vectors, which look like arrows. It is important to know the differences. The force should be generated in a straight direction and should be equal to the charge of the body going through targets, kicking and punching. It is always felt when you hit a hard target such as a punching bag or makiwara board. The more force placed on the object, the more energy it requires, and the more energy is returned.

It is a fact researched by thousands of engineers, scientists, and architects that the human body, using an attack such as hammer fist, knife hand or kick delivered from a flexed knee, results in an increase of total impact force. By adding the upper shoulder and pushing the force down using the hand, needed speed is created to prevent injuries as well as to knock the target off balance. Slightly dropping the upper body during any technique definitely increases the strength of the attack, but it also changes its direction. Therefore we must control effectively the attack as we are approaching impact.

The flexibility of the combined stance and the anatomical back strength of a fighter or martial art trainee give a solid edge in balance. Do not arch the back! Flex the waist and that will deflate the oncoming force. Force cannot exist without acceleration and energy; speed will be demanded for an attack. The greater the speed of attack the less chance of injury to the attacker's body parts, especially the forehead. They are directly proportional. Speed and body force are very important for all martial artists to recognize. Speed is absolutely necessary for a successful attack. If we hit a target without speed, focus, energy and power, we will not be able to penetrate the target. The faster the impact, the more energy will go into the target before it can move away. It is obvious when the target can move.

When kicking a solid surface, if we do not use power combined with speed, the target will not move. Slowing the energy and power you will be unable to penetrate the target or the attack. The effect can also be seen in breaking boards, blocks and glass, especially when it is needed. By increasing the speed and power there will be no need for too many holders in breaking with a side kick, roundhouse kick, and so on. Two holders will be sufficient for a successful break. Research has proven for instance that a shoulder push from a side position, if not using proper speed combined with force and power, will not move the opponent. The angle of attack is very important also, to avoid loss of power through deflection. Of course, to absorb the pain all martial artists in fighting or breaking must develop their inner strength with a strong kiaa or yaa. One of the most perfect examples of using mass is in the flying side kick where the martial artist is forced to combine acceleration. The position of the body to aim and strike, penetrating through behind the target 's successful execution.

It is quite possible the harder the martial artist focuses on energy and speed that his executions are still not successful. The more effort, the more focus will decrease the results. Acceleration of speed is vital, resulting in efficiency of power delivery with the same effort, but with greater speed successful completion especially in free fighting styles, self defense, breaking and so on.

Many different martial arts grand masters practitioners, especially tae kwon do, power, speed and force factors, have been shown in movies. Bruce Lee and other movie stars showed that a bigger man, a more heavy man, is not more powerful than the lighter fighter.

It has been proven that the fighter who is in better condition and uses speed combined with power is always successful against a heavier opponent. The heavier fighter is slower on execution of techniques, self-defense, blocking and motion of movements. The focus of the power is extremely important, with the combination of speed, to overpower a massive fighter.

For example, a martial artist trains with weights to develop a bigger body. He will not successfully overpower the lighter martial artist who uses speed workout, punching, kicking wall targets, hand targets, etc. Because of that body difference, the lighter of the two is freer to activate the energy and force needed with speed for execution to a successful win. Children student martial artists must be made aware of these scientific facts and their potential, especially as they learn to fight large opponents.

Many people say the value of a martial artist is defined by what he has done. First of all, he is as good as the number of people he has competed against. All the best martial artists have learned that their practice of the martial arts is not always a competitive struggle. It is obtaining discipline and awareness and learning to control that which is within us that makes us more humane and sensitive to others.

Competition is good for all of us. It transforms the winners and dismisses the losers, opening doors for success. But this must be done simultaneously, instilling a sense of modesty, courtesy and integrity into a student. The basics of the martial arts start from the basic stance all the way to the investment of our mind in the forms. We must cultivate a mentality of the best of each individual, we must develop and nurture a positive attitude towards life, towards learning, and towards winning and losing.

Section IV

A BRIEF NOTE ON FORMS

Forms are the ways of martial arts.

FORMS

The purpose of forms is that of a basic format of experience, the techniques and exercises to prepare patterns for fighting practice. In forms, a martial artist trains to perform all basic techniques: blocking, punching and kicking in all directions, so that he will be able to defend against many opponents. Practice of the form helps the martial artist control accuracy, balance, endurance and in developing these, also enables him to become proficient and disciplined. A practitioner must consider the movements and essential elements of performance, especially in tae kwon do.

All forms in martial arts are preset movements created through many generations and taught throughout all schools in the world. The martial artist has the chance to practice not only the vision, but the speed, balance and coordination as he turns in different directions to perform and execute the required motions. The patterns in forms differ from one form to another and each form has basic blocking, basic stance increasing in difficulty to blocking, punching, kicking techniques and turning techniques. Each category of each form is conceived by a particular view point and there are different types that are required for martial artists to advance in rank.

In tae kwon do style, beginners, white belts to yellow belts, are required to study the kicho forms, kicho 1-3. They include basic performance of low blocks, solid middle punches, high punches, high blocks, front stance, back stance, horse stance, middle blocks, low blocks, and the turning motions for each sequence applied.

As the martial artist progresses to advancing levels, there are the palgwe 1-8. Palgwe forms have an addition of kicking techniques combined with blocking execution of knife hand punches, middle blocks, self-defense motions and difference stances, i.e., back stance, horse stance, front stance, cat stance, tiger stance. All these forms are in preparation to further develop accuracy, speed and balance as you progress toward your black belt and ranking.

Then there are the eight taegeuk forms, intended for the mental as well as the physical training of the tae kwon do practitioner, combining basic movements with philosophy to stimulate and encourage good mental balance between martial arts skills and the traditional values of tae kwon do. In the taegeuk form all stances are basic except there are high stance instead of low and combined with low stance throughout the progress of the high taegeuk forms. The movements in taegeuk forms differ in execution as far as blocking, kicking and turning motions, which are to symbolize thunder and courage needed to face danger. Some forms have a forceful technique, others a gentler one like water characterizing constancy and flow with its motion. Certain motions teach the stop at a particular step, suggesting the wisdom of knowing where and when to stop. All forms are preparation for fighting, self-defense, and execution of all techniques taught through every day practice at a martial art school.

A martial artist in forms has the chance to show his ability to a grand master all the techniques he has been taught. It is his challenge to perform to his highest ability. Not only for events and promotion examinations but for every day and every time he is at the gym. A martial artist has to continuously work on his fundamental basic execution of hand, foot and leg techniques as well as turning speed, including turning the head and eyes, to all necessary directions.

That is what the forms are all about: preparation for self-defense, technique, and one step sparring where martial artists face each other and work on the different execution of the techniques that are taught through forms. By executing the forms well and knowing the level that is required in the education of the forms, a martial artist advances through testing to high levels. The more time the martial artist invests in the forms and basic workouts, the better his chances to remember and perform well in championships. In doing the forms, he also learns the form's philosophies, including how it was created and where that motion will be applied against an opponent. Techniques demonstrated by a master teacher and learned will advance the martial art student to higher levels because of the experience he gains through the basic practice of forms, fighting, self-defense, one-step sparring and combination techniques.

Martial artists should study well all their techniques, visualize all their basic ideas and practice the breaking as well as performance techniques in front of a master and grand masters. They should be able to improvise and always be willing to study and go back and work on the basics. That is the only way a martial artist can execute outstanding techniques in fighting as well as breaking. *The confidence and the will power for success is being the best you can be.*

DIRECTION LINE OF MOVEMENT

PYONGWON

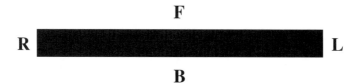

Form

1   2   3

Pyongwon

The coordinate movements in forms symbolize the simple power and connection to earth. It also symbolizes the end of the day where a man's spirit should be filled with that he has acquired or accomplished that day. Conserve, reunite, translate power and spirit to grace and flexibility.

1 Start in choombe stance, feet together, feet in ready stance, arms bent, slightly, tight fists.

2 Same stance, open palms, place left hand on top of right.

3 Open feet one step apart, cross arms in front of chest. Slowly execute knife hand blocks simultaneously down to sides.

4 From low knife hand position bring both hands up to neck level. Slowly push outward, keeping your hand at face level and exhale.

5 Shift your balance. Turn 90 degrees to left leg back stance, cross right arm and execute single low knife hand block.

6 Same back stance, turn and face right leg forward. Shift left leg 90 degrees to left for right back stance while simultaneously executing a single left hand middle block.

7

8

9

7 Change stance to left forward stance. Swing elbow right arm upward to face level, bring left fist to left hip.

8 With right leg execute a front snap kick.

9 Drop right leg and quickly follow up with a turning back kick using left leg.

10 Execute a back kick.

11 Drop your left leg down, slide right foot 90 degrees to your right. Assume a right back stance simultaneously executing a right hand middle block.

12

13

14

12 Same stance circle both hands over your head.

13 Execute a right knife hand low block.

14 Raise both fists and execute double hand high block. Shift balance on left foot. Raise right foot, assume horse back stance, execute back fist strike with right arm to the chin. Bring left fist under right elbow parallel to the floor.

15 Same stance. Shift balance to your right foot. Raise left foot while reaching behind with left hand, stomp down with left foot and execute a back fist upper cut to the chin. Bring right fist under left elbow.

16 Cross over right foot with left foot. Assume an X stance while executing with both elbows outward strike facing left.

17 Move right foot to the right. Cross both fists together at face level and snap them out to the side. Bend elbows half way.

15

16

17

18 Keep left foot in place. Bring your right foot to left knee and assume a crane stance while simultaneously executing left arm high block, right arm low block

19 Bring your right leg to side kick position.

20 Execute a side kick with right foot.

21 Bring right foot down to a right front stance and simultaneously execute an elbow strike with left arm to the chin.

22 Execute a front snap kick with left leg.

23 Step forward with left foot, shift balance and immediately pivot 180 degrees clockwise.

21

22

23

24 Execute back turning kick with right leg.

25 Bring right foot down. Face left and shift foot 90 degrees to left. Hands together execute a left knife hand middle block.

26 Same stance. Raise both arms in a large circle above the head.

27 Execute a left knife hand low block.

28 Raise both arms and execute double hand high blocks, shift left foot to face forward.

26

27

28

29

30

31

29 Shift balance to right foot. Raise left foot and reach behind with left hand.

30 Assume horse back stance. Stomp down with left foot. Execute a back fist with left arm to the chin.

31 Same stance, bring right fist back.

32 Stomping right foot down. Execute a right back fist while in horse back stance.

33 Step with right foot over left foot while executing a double elbow strike outward.

34 Keep right foot in place and assume a horse stance. Execute with both arms crossing in front of your face a spread snap block face left.

32

33

34

35 Assume a crane stance, pick up left leg. Place by right knee, high block with right arm and low block with left arm.

36 Bring left foot and place by right knee.

37 Execute a side kick with left foot.

35

36

37

38 Bring kicking leg down one step forward into a left front stance. Simultaneously execute an elbow strike with right arm shoulder level.

39 Shift left foot 90 degrees facing forward and bring right foot next to left foot. Cross open left hand over right hand.

40 Shift left leg to the left side one step apart. Make fist and assume chōōmbē stance.

190

Section V

BREAKING

Breaking: Demonstration of power, focus, speed, energy, skills, talent and outstanding fists.

CHAPTER 1

What Is the Dynamic Art of Breaking?

Breaking is the most explosive and fascinating subject of martial arts. Dynamic demonstrations by the world's best breakers greatly impress spectators. Breaking is widely practiced in tae kwon do. Literally, tae kwon do is the art of kicking and punching. It is a native form of fighting, which originated in Korea. The fighting system in tae kwon do consists of kicking, punching, blocking, ducking and parrying. It is a system that works the entire body: lower, middle and upper. It is an all around system, in which practitioners must develop their entire body to perform the tae kwon do techniques. These skills and body development come from regular attendance at a tae kwon do school run by great masters.

Breaking is also practiced in other martial art forms: karate, jujitsu, sho-do-kan, Japanese style, kung fu. In modern times, hand techniques have become increasingly important in the world of martial arts. Use of the feet however remains the trademark and the beauty of the tae kwon do style. Tae kwon do students have to practice and devote substantial time on development of the leg muscles, hip and back for performance of these kicks. The first step in training is stretching exercises specifically designed to limber the entire body. Certain stretches focus on certain muscle groups. Developing their stretch and strength to the fullest enables the student to master the positions of tae kwon do.

My Grand Master, Dr. Richard Chun, 9th degree black belt and a champion, asked me to write a book to summarize my knowledge and experience as gained through my training with him and other Masters in the martial arts.

I have experienced many competitions against the world's best fighters and breakers. After almost six hundred championship competitions, I am ranked one of the world's best master breakers. This book comes from thirty-two years of gathered competitive experience and knowledge in breaking and from daily practice and devotion to the martial arts.

The first time I performed a breaking technique in public, I injured myself. I attempted to break a piece of a tree with a hammer fist. I almost broke my hand.

Studying with the world's best breakers I have learned breaking techniques, history, philosophy, training. Breaking is the ability to go through a hard surface such as brick, board, cement blocks, glass, roof tiles, with bare hands, feet and head. Breaking is a power generated from within oneself, focusing great concentration, accuracy, speed, coordination and confidence. All a breaker's internal power is focused on one point, the point of contact between the object he is breaking and his body.

The breaker sets his mind and controls his body while in action. It is a must for the body to lock into position while striking the target and expelling a loud ki-op on contact. Great reflexes are needed for flying techniques, to land safely without injury to oneself or holders. To execute a successful break, every break must be practiced until the positions are perfected, even the steps taken before striking a target. For example, for flying kicking techniques, adjust for the length of the run to the target. The mindset must be positive, never allowing for nervousness or loss of confidence. A successful break is often the result of ambitious, strong will power, positive, confident thinking and repeated competitions. Constant training exercises and stretching techniques are essential. Strength in breaking is the result of speed and accuracy. Speed and the locking of the striking surface provide the force which breaks the target.

As discussed earlier, some striking techniques include the front punch, back fist, hammer fist, spear hand thrust, knife hand strike, ridge hand, palm hand, elbow attacking forward, upward, backward and downward. The most widely practiced elbow break is the strike downward.

The front kick is one of the strongest kicks for breaking. The round house kick, back kick, wheel kick, side kick, crescent kick are done with the outer edge surface of the foot as the striking surface.

A student must be in good physical health and must practice his conditioning as per the previous chapter. The use of targets and striking the surface many times to toughen the areas you wish to use for breaking is very helpful.

Daily kicking practice includes the roundhouse kick, sidekick, and front kick. The constant repetition increases speed, reflexes and strength. Jumping rope will also build speed and reflexes, creating stronger leg muscles for high jumping and turning kicks, which helps the legs become accustomed to the shock of the force of breaking the target.

One of the most helpful exercises to increase stamina is running. It strengthens and stretches the leg muscles. In this book, different subjects are covered which explain the importance and significance of every movement in each technique described along with a stretching exercise for that technique. I will discuss the facts and forces of breaking. People think when they see a martial artist break a hard surface target that possibly it is a trick.

Breaking is part of martial arts training. One must practice to train the body and the mind, to absorb the blow and go through the target. The breaker must look beyond the target to accomplish the difficult breaks, and must do so with absolute confidence.

There are two distinct breaking styles. The most common is the "brutal strength" break done by power breakers. Of course, anyone can perform a simple break with this method, but the consequence of achieving perfection by doing this breaking technique may not be worth it. It may not be safe.

All a power breaker must do is aim at the target on the floor and strike the object, be it wood or cinder block, with extreme force. Unfortunately, as his breaks become more difficult by adding blocks, the more long-term damage to the body results. Good strength in breaking starts and ends with a different kind of power. That is energy+speed+force = power.

Students should not practice breaking without consulting an expert master breaker first. When a martial artist tries to break using his hand, the smallest resistance could stop his power to move through the target. The energy must travel through the target. One must not rely only on strength to go through. As breaking abilities increase, the martial artist starts to use different techniques as well as positions. For example, breaking an empty glass bottle, a very common demonstration in breaking, is not more difficult than breaking a single board.

A common break is soft drink bottles laid flat on their sides and smashed with the hand. Aiming at their large surface area, these bottles are fairly easy to break. Twelve ounce bottles increase the difficulty slightly due the to decreased surface area. Long-necked liquor bottles are usually broken upright with a knife hand technique.

Some martial arts practitioners have found ways to deceive their audiences with spectacular breaking techniques. But challenging breaks performed by jumping, bending, flying sidekicks, or involving the breaking of glass, are difficult techniques to master. These breaks all require great skill and reflex training, as well as physical strength and power from within oneself.

The next chapter begins the process of learning to train the body to perform breaking techniques, which begins with points and advice on breaking.

Chapter 2

POINTS ON BREAKING

CHAPTER 2

Tae kwon do, like every other sport, must be practiced in the correct manner. In earlier chapters, we explained the importance of stretching. It is part of your final goal, to break well.

Breaking is the ultimate test of the martial artist. It demonstrates the skills of one who practices with dedication, showing the ability to break hard surface targets with bare hands and feet using varying techniques.

Children studying the martial arts should not start breaking before eight years of age because the bones and muscles are not yet strong enough. And, after that age, if not supervised by their Master, they may be damaged permanently.

A martial artist should be conditioned, physically and mentally, before attempting to break. Don't jump to conclusions. When you look at an opponent or a target, don't conclude it is easy to do. Whatever you hit is going to exert pressure back at the striking surface of your body. If you hit the floor, resistant pressure from the floor meets your blow and has the potential to cause damage to the body part by "striking it." Any target can do the same.

Begin with soft targets, for example 1/2 inch pine wood in thickness, size 12"x12". Check before breaking a target that it is being held in a position that allows the breaker to break with the grain. This is very important. Before you aim, check your distance. Make certain you are completely ready, begin in a good fighting stance.

Be certain that any point of the body you are using as the striking surface is conditioned for your break, especially when breaking for the first time. Check the distance two or three times before the attempt. Check the movements you will use to break slowly, eye the center of the target. When ready: go through the target, not to the target.

After stretching and before the break, take the time to get your thoughts together, perhaps in a kneeling position with folded arms to mediate quietly. You can mediate anywhere, be it quiet or noisy. During mediation calm your body and mind; bring them both into a quiet controlled state. Approaching breaking nervously or without confidence may result in failure to break. You must focus your physical and mental energies before approaching the targets. Focus your energies upon breaking and nothing else. After meditating, prepare to break.

Begin all breaking techniques with a loud ki-op. This helps to focus the body's strength towards one point, the striking part of the body. Ki-op loudly when striking the target.

It is important to have control over your technique. Be certain you do not injure your holders. If attempting successive breaks, before proceeding to the next target, refocus your concentration quickly. If you are a beginner, place yourself in front of the target and once again: measure your distance, go through the movements you will use to break slowly two or three times, then proceed with the technique. Do not take too long though.

As you progress in breaking, your confidence will grow, but do not expect to succeed all the time. There will be times you will miss your break for various reasons. Sportsmen go through both difficult and easy periods. There are days when everything goes fine for you and then there are days, though no fault of your own, that things do not go right. Hope for tomorrow today, not tomorrow, and do your best now.

If you fail to break, try again but do not be so persistent as to injure your body.

In warmer weather, the body stretches and warms more quickly, but also tires much more easily. In cold weather, keep your legs and feet warm up to the moment you begin your techniques.

As you progress in breaking, prepare physically not only by stretching but by mental preparation. The day before, you must relax. Decide which techniques you want to do and review them in your mind.

During competition, it is very important to maintain a cheerful personality, exchanging conversation with your fellow martial artists. New ideas begin with such exchanges. It is sometimes difficult to understand the way expert breakers do their own unique special techniques, so if you want to learn, ask them about it. Ask questions, broaden your personal knowledge. Do not assume.

In any sport, courtesy to the judges is mandatory. Upon being called before the judges, present yourself in front of the judges in an attentive stance, in a loud, confident voice, announce your school name, your master's name, your own name and the techniques you will be demonstrating. Always bow to the judges and ask permission to begin. Once you have begun, every move is important, there must be no hesitation. If a fellow student has been injured, do not stop your techniques unless specifically indicated by the judges. Anyone injured will be cared for. Continue your techniques, control your mind and your body, concentrate, focus on only breaking, only on what you must do. Do not let surrounding circumstances break your concentration nor your confidence. Concomitantly, when a fellow competitor is successful, do not let this break your concentration either. Everyone has different techniques and abilities and demonstrates them differently.

It is very important to work with the audience, to get their attention. When a dangerous break is about to be done, ask the judges to request silence from the audience. It is very important to concentrate and do your best. Do not rush. Set your station, have your holders ready and explain to them what techniques you will be doing.

Practice all techniques with higher belts in your own school before attempting them in public or in competition. If you have a problem with the break, ask your instructor to show you the technique. It is very important that you know within yourself that you can do the break by having completed it successfully prior to performing it in a championship. Be confident with your techniques.

Be very respectful to fellow martial artists. The respect that you give is returned back to you. Towards higher belts, be humble and open-minded. This is a major asset of learning in the world of martial arts. As time passes, change your patterns and techniques. This will help you grow. It is important to vary breaks, trying different positions, as the different movements will be of value in sparring.

What are the benefits of breaking? This is a frequently asked question.

Breaking is necessary to a point. If you do not want to break, other things may replace this stage of your training. But, if attempted and mastered, the rewards are great in terms of increased self-confidence. Your faith in the strength, skills, speed and accuracy of your personal techniques will improve.

If you are hesitant about breaking in public, practice privately after instruction about the correct technique by a higher belt. You may simply set up two cinder blocks, put pine boards across them (a half inch from each edge of the block) and try to break. The important thing is to try. By trying, you always succeed because no one can accomplish his ultimate if he does not begin by trying.

If family and friends attend a tournament or championship, ignore their presence. Do not think about what you did yesterday or what you will do tomorrow. Think only of the moment and the technique you are about to do. I cannot stress this enough. Always concentrate on what you are about to execute. This will help you achieve the best possible results. Concentrate on the moment; do not avoid it. Yet, don't be overly confident. If you miss on your first attempt, do not stop. Some people start slowly, others more quickly. Find your own individual style and pace. Each person has his own unique knowledge, skills, pace, techniques and abilities. It is up to you to develop your technique to its fullest potential.

Chapter 3

SET UP OF BREAKING STATIONS
And Holders Assistance

a Wood Breaking

Select your wood carefully usually, clear #1 Pine. The grain of the wood should be as wide as possible, so it may have more flexibility. Preferably use wood without knots to avoid injury. Size usually is 12" wide by 12" long or 12" wide by 10" long, by 1" thick. Make sure the board is dry, preferably the ones without a bow in them.

b Most Resistance

Board set up on cement block or held by hand for breaking. The boards should be set to rest approximately 1/2" on each cement block support, with the wood grain to run parallel and the width sides to rest on the block. There are different ways of stacking the boards. There is most resistance when all the boards are placed touching each other. The resistance is increased by the amount of boards being broken. This breaking requires great energy and striking power.

c Mid Resistance

As you use spacers between boards it will decrease the resistance.

d Least Resistance

When using spacers between each board.

a Block Breaking
Cement cinder block should be 8" wide by 18" long by 1³/₄" thick and dry. Place on supports, 1/2" on each side.

b Set Up For Palm Heel Strike.
Shown here are five boards with maximum resistance as they are stacked touching, no space in between. Stand in front stance and shift slightly to your left in order to generate more power from your right shoulder.

c Cinder Block Assistants
Cinder block should be held the long way with the hands holding top and bottom ends. The holders should lean against each other for added support; the cinder block when broken could scatter to many pieces. Place pre cut boards on assistants' insteps to prevent injury.

d Holders Assistants
Holders must know to hold the targets properly. In order to ensure an effective break, target should be held with the fingers only extending over the front of the boards. The arms must be locked to absorb the impact of the break and not pull back or drop the target. Use a front stance that is more stable on the floor.

Chapter 4

HAND BREAKING
TECHNIQUES
and Applications

Front Punch.   Forms Steps 1-4

Side View

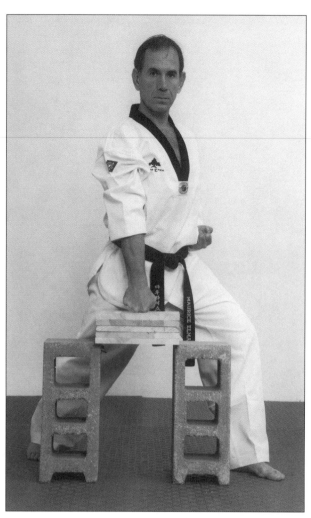

Downward Front Punch - Right

Downward Front Punch - Wrong

Front Punch - Right

Front Punch - Wrong

Punching Stance and Strike

A punch can be practiced from front stance, back stance, and horse back stance. For breaking, the back stance is most commonly used to utilize body weight behind the strike. Hand and hip movements must be coordinated to coordinate the maximum power thrusts to penetrate the target. As the punch is delivered, the back foot pivots and the hip shifts to forward positions distributing 60 degrees of the body weight to the front foot with an additional force behind the punch. The shoulders then face forward from a 45 degree angle of the back stance to 180 degrees front. Keep upper body straight and center shift your gravity forward by pivoting on ball of back foot and shifting leg to the side, opening up to a front stance. Keeping the fist tight, move fist from hip position, tucked tightly close to body, then extend the arm 80 to 90 degrees forward. Twist your hand into the target palm down, with relaxed shoulder to fully incorporate speed and power behind the punch. The forefinger and middle finger knuckles should be the only points of contact, the only knuckles that are in direct line with which to support the wrist and to avoid injury. Do not make contact with the ring finger and the little finger knuckle as it is definitely the wrong way.

I suggest breathing exercises in between each break. Stand with palms open, raise arms above head, inhaling as you raise your hands. In a wide motion push hands down toward trunk of body and exhale. This releases extra oxygen stored in your body. Repeat this exercise two times in between each break and/or exercise.

a Assume a back stance

b Set up your boards and arrange for proper distance. Focus with tight fist and aim to center of board which is the point of impact.

Front Punch Break

c Follow through the break with full arm extension beyond the boards. At this point transfer the power generated from the shift of stance forward with a very loud yaa to absorb the pain. Do not pull the punch back until the boards are broken and the punch has gone through and beyond.

a, b, c, d, e, f

Applications: Reverse front punch to capitalize on a counterattack. You must strike at the same height with a fast reflex action. Coordinate blocking and punching to open targets. Focus is a must, using speed to penetrate.

Wrist Hand   Form Steps 1-3

a Start with wrist bent and exposed forward at hip level. Keep your left hand by your chest.

b Shift your stand to a full front stance, simultaneously extending your striking wrist forward to target, middle section. Bring back your left hand and place it by your hip.

c Repeat same for wrist strike to face level and use an upward motion to the chin.

d Application
Thrust wrist hand into opponent's chin, lock your elbow to generate more power upon resistance.

a Wrist Break

Repeat same as front punch. Use the back of the wrist. Set up the target with holders. Bring all fingers and thumb together.

b Focus and aim wrist to center of target. Bend hand with fingers inward to expose outer wrist surface.

c, d Using a twisting motion of hips, thrust forward
with speed for more energy. At point of thrust, extend
your arm, with strong yaa. Lock elbow at completion
of follow through.

Hammer Fist Downward Strike   Form Steps 1-4

a Make fist with both hands, start in back stance.

b Raise striking hand upwards above your shoulder.

c Face bottom surface of fist down, start to strike toward target in arc motion, change your stance to front stance.

d Snap striking hand downward using speed to increase power with the help of your shoulder.

Side View 1-2

Hammer Fists

This is an excellent technique for breaking, blocking and fighting. Often known as the most powerful downward strike, used on legs, head and elbow. Make a fist, use surface of the outer edge of fist, position your hand by hip and start with back stance, facing the target. Swing the arm in a circle by bringing it behind your back over your shoulder. The arm should be extended with the elbow slightly bent. Use your entire weight for the downward thrust. Shift back leg to side to complete your front stance. Focus on target and use speed with power as you twist the upper shoulder to complete the strike.

a, b Hammer Fist Break
Set up cinder block with holders. You also can use a support block on the floor.
Start with back stance, focus your mind and aim to center point of target.

c Aim your hammer fist to center of cinder block. Concentrate on the bottom of the fist.

d Twist the upper body in the direction of the target, shift leg to the side for front stance, thrust with strong yaa through the target.

215

Applications

a Strike with hammer fist downwards to the clavicle.

b As opponent grabs the shirt follow up with a hammer fist strike, bringing your hand from the outside to the temple.

c Use a hammer fist block downward to block front kick strike to middle section. The fist should follow through in order to slow the power of the kick and push the leg to the side.

d Strike with hammer fist downward to forehead.

216

Knife Hand

The second most effective strike after the reverse punch is the knife hand, used for attacks to the neck, face, ribs, temple, head and abdomen. It is great for blocking leg kicks and weapons. Knife hand may be used with palm up or down, the striking point the outer edge of the hand between the wrist and pinkie finger. It should be strengthened with wall targets or a maki-wara board to develop calluses so the frag-ile bones of the hand are able to absorb the shock at point of impact. The little finger should not make contact with the object being struck, because of its great sensitivity. Start from back stance, raise your hand across chest above your shoulders and strike across, into the target. Twist your hand slightly, with the elbow pulled in toward the body just before impact, in order to increase the force and the speed of the knife hand. Fingers must be held tightly so they do not separate on impact to increase the force and speed of the knife hand. Knife hand can be used to strike down, inward and outward. When breaking with knife hand, to success-fully accomplish a break, you must coordi-nate strength, technique, and motion of movements in good timing.

a

b

Diagram for Knife Hand Strike to Middle Section Chest and Neck
Form Steps 1-4

a Open knife hand in back stance, keep right elbow parallel to floor. Left hand open knife position.

b Raise your right hand above the shoulder.

c As you start to strike, twist right hand and continue motion downward in arch from shoulder.

d Snap right hand, twisting the wrist with speed to increase the power on the blow and simultaneously switch to front stance.

c

d

Knife Hand Strike

a

b

a Assistants should hold the boards firmly, with locked arms, in front stance. Check holders resistance by pushing with your hands against the boards. Find the perfect angle for the strike and rehearse a few times.

b Pick your knife hand above the shoulder and aim to point of focus.

c

c With strong yaa, swing the arm and shoulder, using all your body weight to strike the boards without hesitation and follow through the break. Don't pull the hand back until break is completed.

Knife Hand Applications

a

b

a Knife hand block against a punch. Could be used for high, middle or low.

b Striking knife hand to the abdomen or chest.

c Stepping out, striking knife hand to the back of neck.

d Repeat same as knife hand break. Striking knife hand to the neck with right hand, block kick with left hand.

e Knife Hand Strike to Temple
As opponent strikes with front punch, shift your stance to your left and strike with knife hand to the temple.

c

e

d

Knife Hand Strike Downward
to High Middle and Low Areas   Form Steps 1-4

a Start from back stance, open knife hand.

b Raise your right hand above your shoulder near your ear.

c Face edge of right hand down. Start to strike toward target in arch motion. Keep your left hand by your chest.

d Snap and twist right hand as it travels downwards. Change your stance to front stance and use speed to increase power with the help of your shoulder.

Application

e Block opponent's strike, use knife hand downward strike to elbow.

f Downward knife hand side view.

Knife Hand Strike Down Glass Fire Break

The following glass break should be performed with the supervision of an experienced martial art master. The author and publisher will not be responsible for any accidents or injuries sustained during the execution of any break shown in this book.

Knife Hand Downward Strike

Start with back stance facing forward with target set up in front. Raise your hand above your shoulder, elbow parallel to floor. When you begin the strike downward toward the target, you will need to meditate, concentrate, and focus on the break. The mind and body must act together. When you are ready, swing the knife hand quickly, switch to front stance, keep the elbow bent as you make contact to avoid excess pressure on the joint. Keep fingers tight and upon impact keep lowering your stance to continue the break. For this break you can use a baseball bat, pinewood, bricks, cinder block, slate roof shingles, 2"x4" wood, etc.

The following glass firebreak is for demonstration purpose only.

Back Fists

Form Steps 1-3

a Application
For back fist strike, use a very fast snap on the attack and aim accurately for strike to the jaw.

b Strike to opponent's chin using the first two knuckles, striking with back hand fist, delivering in downwards direction from outside to chin area.

Back Fists

Start with back stance. Bend your wrist and use back of fist to make contact only with the back of the first two knuckles. Bring the striking hand to opposite ear. Bend your arm across the chest. Focus and start to shift your front leg by lifting the leg to your outside (if using right hand, shift leg to right side). Snap the back fist forward towards the target, twist your fist backward and strike target with the first two knuckles, keep elbow bent, upper body straight and coordinate your arm snap, body and leg movement, with all the body power concentrated on the back fist. Follow through the break.

a Back Fist
This is effective in strikes to the temple of the head. Face and position yourself by target. Swing the back fist across your chest as far as you can over your head.

b Strike the target in the center with the first two knuckles.

c Strike with back fist approaching the target with a loud yaa. Use your shoulder to build up more power.

d The back fist must follow through the break, maintaining a very tight fist.

Hammer Fist Strike Sideway   Form Steps 1-4

To ribs, chest, side of temple, same direction and position as knife hand outside to inside

Application

Use a side thrust hammer fist with the control to strike opponent's rib cage, while blocking opponent's high punch.

Hammer Fist Break Sideway

a

a Make a tight fist, use ony the outer edge surface of fist. Aim at target with twisted shoulder.

b Thrust target by moving hammer fist with great speed from outside position to inward, strike in circle motion.

c Thrust hammer fist into center of target with strong yaa, speed and power. Control blow to avoid contact with holders.

b

c

Palm Heel Strike Outward

If the palm hand is used with right angle, with the support of the shoulder it should be a stronger strike than the punch because it does not have fragile bones. Palm heel strike can be used for downward, upward and outward strike with the use of body weight and the shifting from back stance to front stance. From back stance, open palm heel, start to travel from hip toward the target and upon impact lock elbow for solid resistance while shifting your stance from back stance to front stance.

Form Steps 1-3

Palm Heel Break

a

a Set up target at proper height with holders. For more boards use second holder to support elbows of first holder. For better resistance, adjust distance. Start from back stance.

b Aim, focus at center of target, twist hip forward.

b

c Thrust striking palm heel into target by driving hand through target.

d Repeat same technique for palm heel outward strike.

c

d

Applications Palm Heel Outward Strike

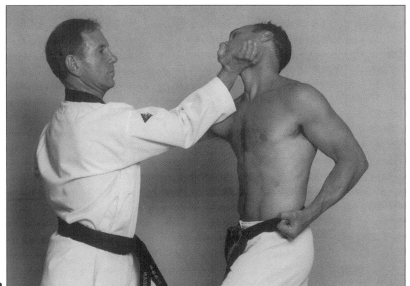

a When opponent starts to move find exposed area for counterattack. With great speed and strength, use palm heel to strike side of opponent's chin.

b Repeat same technique as above for upward strike under opponent's chin or jaw. Thrust hip forward to help the striking hand drive through the jaw.

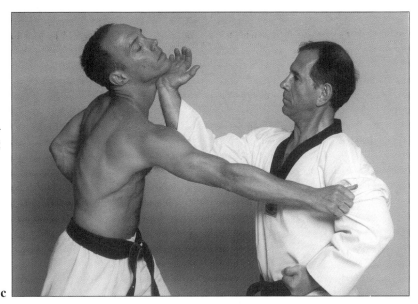

c As opponent grabs your shirt, immediately counterattack the exposed striking areas: face, chest, ribs and neck.

Spear Hand
Form Steps 1-4

Front and Side View

230

Spear Hand

Open your hand and hold fingers firm, thumb curled inward. Bend the second finger to line up with the others. Always keep nails trim to prevent injuries to yourself and others. Striking area is finger tips. As you strike with spear hand from fighting back stance, start execution from the hip with palm up, moving forward. Place opposite hand by the hip. Use striking hand with speed, twist the wrist, and shift to front stance. Extend the arm until spear hand reaches full extension. You must coordinate body, speed, power and stance as you strike target. It is a very difficult and powerful break so you must condition the finger tips with a makiwara board, sand box or rice box. Thrusting the fingers into sand box up to the knuckles trains the fingertips to meet resistance. Wash hand in ice water and repeat many times. Keep fingers straight out with joints locked at time of impact to prevent them from bending inward. This break requires meditation, focus, no hesitation, coordination of body, shoulder and hand. You must know the correct areas and vulnerable targets of attack.

Review the next applications for target areas.

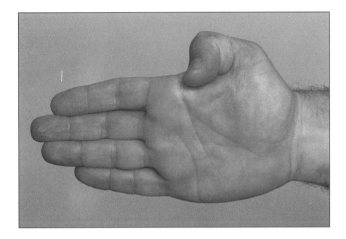
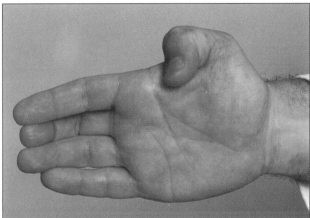

a Wrong   **b Right**

Practice

To condition the fingers you could use a pail filled with sand. Drive the hand with all fingers aligned into the sand pail up to the knuckles. Finger joints will build more strength by meeting resistance. Keep middle fingers in and hold all finger joints in locked position for a successful break.

a Speed Spear Hand
Hold board with one hand. Bring striking spear hand to hip.

b Focus and aim to center of target with strong yaa as you prepare to strike.

c Release the board. Strike with great speed while changing from back stance to front stance. Use the shoulder to add power enough to cause both ends of the board to split in half and fly away.

232

Applications

a Spear Hand strike to under the chin.

b Spear Hand strike to Adam's apple.

c Wrong way - Spear Hand strike to solar plexus.

d Right way - Spear Hand strike to solar plexus.

a

b

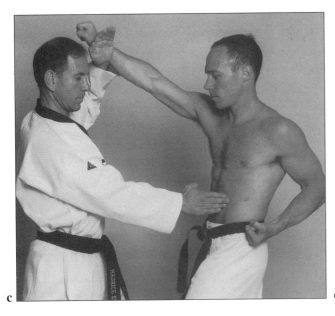

c

d

233

Upward Ridge Hand

Start from back stance middle knife hand, bring striking right hand and place it by the hip. Start to swing right hand in circular motion over your head and behind your back to gain power. As you thrust upward with ridge hand use more speed and shift to front stance by taking one step with right leg sideway. All moves in this technique must be coordinated: the hip, ridge hand, change of stance, speed in order to control the arm stop with ridge hand upward at groin level. It can be used to break an elbow or for self defense.

Form Steps 1-3

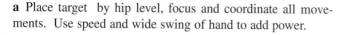

a Place target by hip level, focus and coordinate all movements. Use speed and wide swing of hand to add power.

b Point of impact break through the target.

Ridge Hand Inward

Form Steps 1-4

1

2

3

4

Inward Ridge Hand

Effective blow to the head, neck, abdomen, groin and face using the inner edge of the forefinger knuckles with thumb bent down against the palm, palm face down. From back stance place your ridge hand by hip. Start to swing arm in slight horizontal arch with palm face down as you approach the target. Use shoulder and twist the wrist so hand will thrust through the boards with a snap. Change your stance facing the target as you strike to generate more speed and power, causing the board to fly from the holders.

a Inward Ridge Hand Break
Start with striking hand at hip. Snap ridge hand palm down toward the target in arch outward.

b
Snap ridge hand with the thrust through the boards. With strong yaa, use your shoulder to generate more speed and power. Repeat same for outward strike with palm up. Upward blow to groin.

a

b

236

Ridge Hand Applications

a Block opponent's striking fist with your ridge hand under opponent's elbow. Create pressure by pushing down on opponent's blocked extended arm.

b Block opponent's punch with left hand high block and repeat ridge hand upward from steps 1-3 for groin strike.

c Ridge hand strike to the neck. Block your opponent's punch with high block left hand. Use inward ridge hand with wide swing to gain maximum speed and power to strike the neck.

d Repeat same strike to the temple, nose, face and throat.

a

b

c

d

Thumb Break

(This break is not recommended until it is completely perfected with the help of experienced masters).

The inner first joint is used in the thumb break technique. This joint must be strengthened with push ups or punching bag to develop the ligaments and muscles necessary to absorb the shock of the blow. It is a very impressive technique because of its extreme level of difficulty.

Speed Thumb Break

Start with high stance. Rest board on left hand finger tips. Arm must be extended. Bring striking right thumb from the hip in arch behind your back and over your shoulder. Twist the thumb slightly before approaching the target. Do not strike the thumb directly downward. You **must** twist slightly in order to absorb the entire shock of the blow, otherwise thumb will break.

As you approach the target with the thumb, concentrate your focus with a strong yaa.
Center your power to the thumb and with great speed snap through the board while releasing your supporting
hand to enable the board to split in half in mid air.

Applications

a As opponent strikes with a punch or a kick, shift your stance side ways and use your right thumb in a wide circle downward to the clavicle.

b Repeat same with right hand thumb in outward direction to side of neck below the ear.

c Block opponent's punch with high knife hand block. Use left hand thumb in circle motion upward to strike under the jaw. Keep the thumb firm.

Speed Punch Hand Break

The purpose of speed hand break is to develop power and penetration. The snap of the fist, combined with speed and power, can break through the target with a strong thrust. Focus and concentration at the center of the target is very important in speed breaking. Keep your shoulders at ease at point of impact. Simultaneously pivot your hip. Changing from back stance to front stance, strike forward with the fist, using the first two knuckles as striking surfaces.

Start by holding target with one hand face level, stay in back stance, with striking hand placed by your hip. Perfect timing is essential. Strike the dropped target in mid-air with your fist. This strike demands great speed and power. Upon impact do not stop! Extend your shoulder forward and twist your hip, switch from back stance to front stance. Keep the fist travelling through the target and lock your elbow for suspended breaks to send the target flying to pieces. Most martial art styles use speed hand technique to face, chest, ribs and solar plexus.

Elbow Strike

Applied with thrusting motion in straight line forward. The power is generated by the twisting motion of the shoulder and upper body and should include the arm movement at full speed and power for a successful break.

Form Steps 1-3

a Start by adjusting your distance between target and elbow. Aim at center of target with striking bend elbow.

b From front stance swing striking elbow out to inward with great speed and strong yaa. Thrust target with full arm extension for successful break.

Elbow Strike Downwards

Elbow strike downwards is the most common used technique in breaking for both beginners and advanced students. For downward or back elbow thrust, bend the arm at a 90 degree angle to obtain maximum contraction from the longer triceps muscle located approximately 1" past the elbow joint. Make fist or open knife hand, keep palm toward shoulder. Raise your arm high and keep it near the rear. When you are ready to strike, bring your elbow down in a vertical line to the target. Practice first coordinating the shoulder and properly dropping the arm with the body in a perfect swing downward to achieve greater impact. Do not use the elbow joint itself because of its fragility.

Breaking Target With Elbow Backward

The arm should be parallel to the floor. The strike begins with the elbow travelling directly in front of chest and backward to target with speed, strong yaa and power. Repeat same for upward strike using shoulder muscles for maximum thrust and power.

The following elbow glass break is for demonstration purposes only. You should use wood, cinder blocks or bricks.

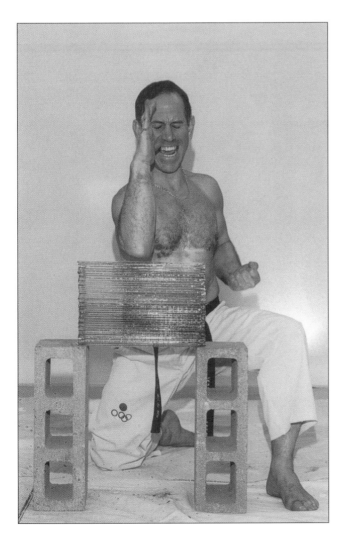

Application

a Elbow strikes

Elbow techniques can be used as strikes to the face, neck, back of head, under chin, chest, shoulders and back.

Elbow strikes can be used as a weapon for defensive breaking of legs and arms.

Elbow Strike Applications

Application on Strike

a Shift your front stance sideways. Grab opponent's striking hand and use upper cut elbow to strike under the chin.

a

b

b If opponent grabs your hip or chest, bring your left hand over the back of his head. Take him off balance by pulling his upper shoulder forward and down strike.

c Step out of opponent's striking punch by shifting your stance sideways and use and outward elbow strike to the jaw.

d Grab opponent's reverse striking hand and use an inward elbow strike to the jaw.

c

d

Double Elbow Strike Backward

Both arms should be equal in strength and speed. Your upper body should be well developed as one of your strongest areas. It is easy to develop an exercise program for upper body development and, commensurately, elbow strike.

a Prepare both targets with holders at proper distance for both elbows to land at center of targets.

b Cross both hands across the chest at shoulder level and simultaneously strike with both elbows outward strike to center of the targets. Continue your motion beyond the targets for a successful break.

c Application
As opponents grab you from behind, immediately strike with both elbows to the ribs, chest and face areas. As they move away from your elbow strikes, take one step backward to reach your target.

a

b

c

Chapter 5

BREAKING WITH LEGS
and Kicking Techniques

Front Kick
Form Steps 1-3

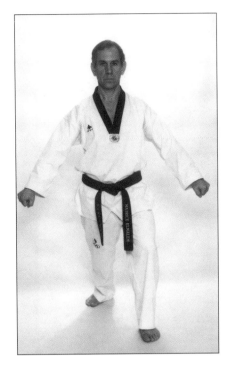 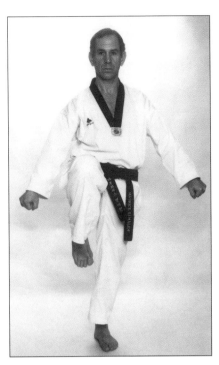 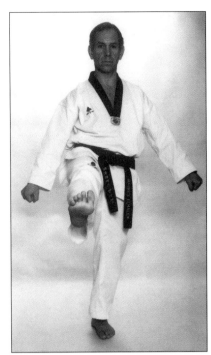

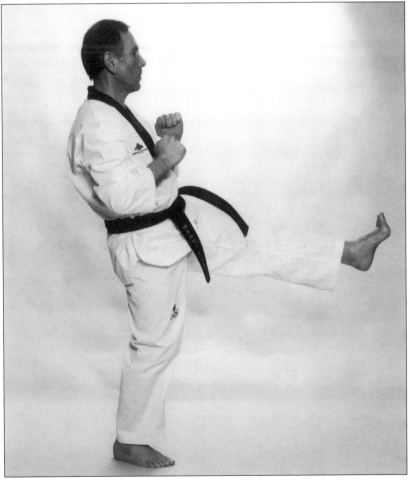

Front Kick Side View

Front Kick

This is the most common breaking kick for both beginners and advanced martial artists. It is a very powerful kick. In fighting it is usually accomplished by a thrusting movement, bringing the leg up from the floor, aiming the knee at the target and snapping the leg using the ball of the foot for striking. Use the hip and aim at center of targets for maximum power on each kicking movement.

a Start from back stance or front stance. Excellent balance and proper distance from the target are essential. Tilt board slightly, use ball of foot, and bend toes back when striking.

b Application
Front kick can be used for attacks to the face abdomen and groin.

c High front kick stretch with the help of an assistant.

Front Kick - Right - Use Ball of feet **Front Kick - Wrong**

d As you snap the leg, thrust into target with a strong yaa. Extend hip forward simultaneously as ball of the foot makes contact. Continue through the target with locked knee, using all the power generated from the mind into the body.

251

Round House Kick
Form Steps 1-4

1

2

3

a

b

Applications
a Roundhouse kick with ball of foot strike to face.

4

b Roundhouse kick strike with instep to face.

Roundhouse Kick

Start in back stance, raise back leg parallel to floor with all your weight on the standing leg. Swing the kicking foot in a circular motion to the target with the foot at a slight angle facing downwards. Curl toes in and use ball of the foot. Snap the kicking foot with full extension to the target. Bring leg back quickly, bend knee and return foot to the floor. Repeat same for use of the instep. Round house kick to the face, ribs, knees and neck.

a Have boards held facing directly forward, tilted slightly inward, step to the side of target. Check holders for resistance.

b Check for proper distance and stance. Stay in back stance.

c Aim ball of the foot at center of the target. Make certain to bend your toes.

a

b

c

d

Focus as you bring kicking leg up. Start to pivot toward the target, foot together with hip and kicking leg. Thrust the ball of the foot into the target with knee locked, strong yaa, and great speed. After breaking the boards, bring kicking foot back to floor.

d

Application

As opponent strikes with a reverse punch, simultaneously move outside of opponent's strike with roundhouse kick to open target; stomach, or abdomen.

Twist Kick
Form Steps 1-4

Twist Kick

This is the only kick to penetrate through the double blocking hands because of the twist angle that the kick is positioned in with a strike from out to in motion. The target is not facing directly in front, but possibly as much as 45 degrees to the side. The kicking leg simultaneously snaps, thrusts, twists and strikes with the ball of the foot. This kick is effective against vital areas such as face, ribs solar plexus and abdomen.

a

b

a Set target facing front. You should be in back stance at a 45 degree angle to target. Aim ball of foot at center of target. Check distance.

b, c Keeping knee slightly bent, snap kick and thrust ball of foot towards center of target. Return leg, knee and foot in same thrusting motion after completion of kick to avoid knee injury.

c

Instep Twist Kick

Repeat same as twist kick using the instep bone of the foot. This kick can be used as a front instep kick. Facing opponent directly, start from back stance or front stance, bring kicking leg up, bend knee forward, point toes down and snap leg upward to target. Extend kicking leg to strike target. Maintain good balance.

a Application Instep Twist Kick
To the face with locked knee against defense.

b Application Twist Kick
To stomach to break through a double block.

c Thrust kicking leg into target using the instep bone of the foot with strong yaa, speed, focus, and co-ordination. All combined for a successful break.

257

Cross Step Side Kick

1 Start with back stance, hands positioned in middle block.

2 Step with left leg to cross in front of right foot, shift weight to left leg.

3 Pick up right leg, bend knee, place kicking leg to middle section above left knee.

Form Steps 1-5

4 Thrust right kicking leg with a snap side kick to face area, place right arm along kicking leg, left hand by chest area.

5 After completion of side kick bring kicking leg back to same ready position.

Side Kick

Form Steps 1-3

Start from back stance. Raise back kicking foot to level of stationary leg, start to pivot leg on ball of foot to the side, at a 90 degree angle so the hip is in line with target. Thrust kicking leg forward, lock knee and use the outer edge of the kicking foot or heel to make contact with the target. As you snap the kicking foot, pivot. The foot moves to align leg with front arm along kicking leg and back arm is positioned at your chest. This motion will increase power on the kick. Shift your upper body toward the kicking leg. Do not bend leg. Use a snap to go through the target. The side kick is an extremely powerful kick. Striking areas include the face, stomach, abdomen. It may be used for blocking.

Hop Side Kick

Start from a horse stance facing the target. Thrust your body forward with a hop by moving back foot forward one step to replace kicking foot. Jump on both feet. Pick up kicking leg off the floor. Bend your knee. Position foot by standing knee of back foot where front foot was. Thrust kicking front foot into target with the help of your hip. Lock your knee and strike through the target, repeat same for high kick. Striking targets are same as side kick.

a Before any break stretch for side kick to avoid muscle cramping.

b Side Kick Strike. Set up the target with holders, for cinder blocks. Use more than one holder. Holding hands must be in lock position. Cover holder's feet with pine wood. They should be in front stance. Instruct holders not to drop remaining cinder block after breaking. They must hold them.

c Add a back up holder. Adjust your distance and aim to center point of the block with striking leg slightly bent to allow for extension through the target.

d As you strike, shift your body weight forward, pivot on your supporting leg at a 90 degree angle, pick up your kicking leg with bent knee and place it by stationary knee. Thrust into target with strong yaa and speed while pivoting on back leg as well to increase the power of the kick.

e Immediately upon the completion of the break, quickly pull back your kicking leg, place it by standing leg to avoid injury.

Application

Side kick to the chest must be under the blocking arms. Move body weight forward and pivot back leg for more power on the kick.

Application

a Side Kick to the Face

Repeat same as middle side kick. Start by raising your kicking leg with bent knee as high as you can. Snap kick to the face.

Application

b You must be two steps away from opponent in order to generate the power when hopping forward. Keep straight line with good coordination of body movements. Snap hop side kick to opponent's chest. Lock your knee.

a

b

Knee Break

Start with back stance. Pick up back leg in a 45 degree angle (same motion as for round house kick). Pivot on standing leg 90 degrees and thrust the knee in arch motion into target. Coordinate the snap, hip, and standing leg movements to generate more power upon impact. The knee can be used straight upward for face target, ribs, chest and groin. Use the knee for self defense as opponent charges in and is about to make contact. Always block striking weapon out of your sight. The knee is very powerful, therefore this technique must be practiced carefully in different directions with good control.

1   2   3   4

Form Steps 1-4

Applications
Use knee strike to opponent's solar plexus, face, ribs, groin as he penetrates defense area. Always strike from side or front.

263

Knee Break

a Start from back stance, check for proper distance, stand to side of target.

b Aim knee at center of the target, touch the boards to test holders' resistance so that assistants don't move backward when strike is executed.

c Thrust knee in arch motion into target with strong yaa.

d Continue knee strike through the target until breaking technique is completed.

Back Kick

Form Steps 1-4

a

b

a Start from back stance.

b While on the floor bend back leg slightly.

c Shift weight on front leg. Pick up back leg. Turn shoulders and body forward with eyes focused on target. Shift your weight to back foot.

d Snap right leg forward. Lean upper body slightly to the back. This kick is useful to the middle section, ribs, chest, face and knees. It is very effective in fighting and breaking.

c

d

Turning Back Kick

Known as the surprise hidden kick, it is very powerful! Start from back stance, pick up your back leg. Turn head and shoulders by pivoting backward on your stationary leg, position the kicking foot straight at the target. Thrust the back kick into the target with the toes curled up, facing down. Extend heel back with clear vision, thrust kicking foot into target. The speed and hip motion will increase the strength of your back kick. Striking points are ribs, abdomen, face, groin, solar plexus.

a

a Start with back stance facing the target. Check on holders, elbows must be locked only exposing the finger tips. From back stance, pick up kicking leg, place it by knee of standing leg. Turn your body, face and shoulders by pivoting backward to face the target.

b Practice - aim at center of target, focus, keep leg slightly bent. Check for proper distance and then return to original stance.

b

c In one continual motion bring back leg up and pivot on stationary leg. Turn your shoulder, look at the target, thrust kicking leg with speed, power and strong yaa into target. Lock your knee.

c

b Turning Back Kick breaking five 1inch boards.

Application

Turning Back Kick – When you are in a fighting stance use as much speed as you can to penetrate the open target.

Turning Hook Kick

a

b

Start from back stance facing target, pivot on front leg, pick up kicking leg with bent knee. Spin with the shoulders and body backwards. As you see the target, thrust kicking foot with speed and power out at target with hook kick backward to strike the target with back heel of the foot. All movements must be coordinated with the entire body.

a From back stance, pick up back leg and pivot on stationary leg. Start to spin.

b Spin backwards and adjust your distance. Aim at center of target. Pivot stationary leg another 90 degrees.

c As you see the target thrust kicking foot with speed and power hook kick backward to strike the target and complete turn to back stance.

d Application
Turning hook kick is effective to the face and chest. The more speed you use for the turning hook kick, the more power is generated on the back of the heel striking surface.

c

d

Heel Down Strike / Heel Stomping

The most powerful kick of the leg techniques. Use the bottom of the heel for stomping. Pick up your striking leg, bend your knee, twist toes and foot up. Shift weight to standing leg, extend arms to the side for balance. Bring heel of kicking leg downwards utilizing coordination of power, hips and upper body. Focus and speed is necessary to accomplish the break with maximum power on the thrusting movement. After completion of the break, quickly return striking leg upward to avoid jamming remainder of target to prevent injuries.

This technique is used for striking to face, chest, abdomen and stomping to any part of the body after a take down.

a The following fire heel stomping is for demonstration purposes only It should only be practiced with the help of an experienced master. First try without fire. Set your target on top of supporting blocks, resting 1/2 inch on each side. Bring striking foot upward, bend your knee, hold on to your balance, and strike down.

b Application
Stomping after a take down to the chest or any part of the body.

269

Thrust your stomping heel to center of target with a strong yaa. Focus, speed and coordination of hip and body are mandatory. Bring your foot upward quickly after strike to avoid injury with jamming broken target.

Wheel Kick

a Check proper height and position of boards with assistants. Boards should be slightly tilted forward in order to avoid injury of back leg with edge of boards while breaking.

b Without bending knee, raise kicking leg in large circular motion moving the foot forward and inward up to above head level with strong yaa.

c Thrust into the target with the heel of right foot forward and downward.

a

d Application

When opponent strikes with front kick and front punch, take one step forward to outside of opponent's front leg. Use a wheel kick strike to the head or chest without bending the knee.

b

c

d

CHAPTER 6

The four most frequently asked questions regarding breaking that I have been asked are:

• Is breaking necessary in the martial arts?

• Do martial artists have to take the dangerous chances they do in the breaking techniques they perform?

• What feelings does breaking generate in the martial artist?

• How can martial arts students achieve breaking techniques without being concerned about the danger?

Breaking is a test of ability whereby martial artists try for their personal best. Personal best is necessary in many aspects of life as well. In each person's life, there are times one must prove oneself against difficulties. Each of us will face problems that require preparation to handle properly. Unless preparation throughout life has strengthened and prepared him, one may find certain problems impossible to solve or handle.

Breakers face these moments. They start to train in the martial arts and move from white belt to higher belts to learn the basics. They begin to comprehend the many dimensions of learning the martial arts. In the tae kwon do style, a martial artist must break to be elevated to certain belt levels. The breaker must prove himself mentally and physically. But, most importantly, he must perform the break he chooses. Breaking is a personal decision. There is no routine as a gymnast has, who must face proscribed challenges.

A martial artist must decide which breaking techniques to perform. Is it the break that will make him look good or the technique? The martial artist has to choose what he can do best. The decision process that the breaker encounters is similar to other day-to-day life decisions.

Breakers always train initially by breaking boards. As they attempt to break these boards, things occur. At first, it can appear very easy. As in other life situations, something can appear as if you can handle it, until you personally face that situation square on. When you break, people are watching: masters, family, judges and others. Everything else must leave your mind except the true martial artist's thought: to do the break and prove one's power. There is a mystique about this concentration. Books, stories, movies have been written about this test a martial artist undergoes to prove his power and concentration. The martial artist stands in front of people trying to prove his strength, power, technique, perfection and most importantly, doing the break he has decided upon.

The body shivers. The mind concentrates solely on breaking, going through the target. Moments like these are frightening.

I remember when I began training. I ran for hours at a time. Sports became the ultimate challenge to me. I realized that to be a good fighter, or a man with a good future, I would have to work very hard. Nothing comes easily. Everything you want and strive for in life comes with hard work and perseverance.

Many other things came to me because of my martial arts training: I became a runner and started entering competitions. First the 100-meter run, then the kilometer, the 5-kilometer, the mini-marathon, and finally, marathons. It took me years to progress, but I enjoyed seeing my growth as a sportsman.

The first time I was exposed to a judo class I was fascinated watching a man being able to defend himself against grabs or attacks and using the power of the body. I wanted to study martial arts, to understand the ability of power within the movements. The mental process impressed me so I began searching for a school where I could study martial arts. I first had to check the different styles and cultures: judo schools, kung fu, karate, etc. The most impressive school I found was one owned by a true Israeli champion, Gidon Cadari, then the current European champion in shodokan.

I began my studies by learning the history of the martial arts. As my studies progressed during the first six months, I developed the understanding that it was absolutely essential to develop my brain, to think about my techniques and how they worked, to become a better gentleman, good fighter, and a top student. To be the best at whatever I was doing. There is no end to proving who you are and what you are as you grow. People build empires by taking chances.

The martial arts have taught me to respect others and strive to do my best. One must only use his or her experience and knowledge in the martial arts when pushed too far.

Today I am in the architectural and design business. I face very important business decisions most days. Breaking and the world of martial arts years have helped me achieve many things.

But, in regards to the martial arts in particular, breaking is the most important subject. A good fighter is always the result of a smart breaker, a result of hard training on a daily basis.

One's first successful break is an exciting accomplishment. Having broken the board and the ability to focus long enough to achieve this result engenders powerful feelings. The person who attempts this learns that when you try to break through a hard surface target, the target gives an equal and opposite force against the striking surface of the body. If the technique is not done well, it hurts. If you are not trained properly, injuries will occur. The successful breaker, most likely, learns this before he or she is successful.

Successful breaking can also be the goal of one's training, but the results of hard training towards building power through strength, speed and accuracy. Students do not always understand how to break hard targets. This can be corrected through information from the Masters and the student's trust. It is worth it - a successful breaker feels like a champion.

In the beginning, one should train with materials that are fairly easy to break, i.e., pine boards. One must build confidence that he or she can go through the target. This confidence comes with hard training. If an attempt at breaking fails, one's confidence may falter and training is set back, sometimes severely so. One must remember first to select materials with a grain. Examples are pine wood, oak, ice, bricks, bottles, glass, concrete blocks. Always make certain it can be broken. Always break with the grain. Aim at the center point of the target.

Boards should be firmly held by fellow students. There must be trust between the breaker and the holders. The grain makes it possible for the object to be broken. Holders should hold along the grain, never against it. This allows the breaker to go through the target.

You should begin with one board and increase the number of boards as you gain confidence and techniques improve. The power from within oneself is a result of one's training. Try to look beyond the challenge. Better yet, formulate an answer or idea in the mind before the problem occurs to save time and avoid extra pressure.

Start easily but be serious. Never forget that to succeed in breaking, the power comes from within. Ask higher belts to help you, but be confident in the techniques before attempting them.

Breaking teaches to take the good with the bad and to accept success and failure. One learns to respect oneself and others. The harder one tries, the better one becomes. It is not difficult unless effort is expended.

Breaking builds reflexes, confidence, and ability. Every time there is a problem in your breaking technique, try to solve it by thinking the problem through. Don't jump to conclusions. That is when people get hurt. Whatever is decided, attempt it with 100% confidence. Then continue to practice and perfect your techniques. Do not attempt any first-time breaks in public. Practice for all demonstrations, first in your school or wherever you train. Then you will have the confidence to perform it in public.

Here are some final thoughts on the subject of breaking. Thinking is the most important skill. That is how championships are won. Never lose your humility. Teach others what you have learned from your masters. Give others a chance to learn by helping them. Be there for other students when they need you. Nothing in the martial arts or life belongs solely to anyone. Share your dream with others. This will make you a true champion. Whatever you decide to learn, try your best. Do not dwell on past mistakes. We are all human; we all make mistakes. We will make more mistakes. To keep trying means to keep making mistakes. Move on.

One needs a strong mental outlook and self-control to succeed. Breaking is the challenge to master power and ability. One must have enthusiasm and a strong will and chance losing to win. Be willing to go beyond one's mistakes to learning from them. Keep practicing. Dreams will stay with you forever.

Chapter 7

PREPARATION FOR FLYING TECHNIQUES

For jumping techniques in competition breaking, after you have registered and completed your warm-up stretch, try the jumping techniques you will do in the tournament, i.e. jumping back kick, jumping front kick, jumping roundhouse kick, etc. Take a target and a chair or something similar and jump over it. This builds your momentum for the moment of your actual flying techniques. Make certain that you lock your legs when performing all techniques. It is often necessary to psyche and focus yourself, to force your body to take charge for a particular technique. So, practice easily and loosely a few times. Do not over exert.

If you select double kicks, make certain both legs are kept warm. You may jump against a wall to adjust the height of your kicks and warm up your legs. Ask holders to position practice targets so you can adjust your height. Position the targets by your own body height, i.e. face, chest, or middle area. Be conscious of your ability to break at the height you choose. Remember there is decreased power with increased height.

For a back kick technique, make sure you are in a fighting stance. Jump straight up. Hit the target straight, despite the initial turning motion. If you keep turning, your striking leg or hand will be in a very weak position to go through the target. Warm up by asking your target holders to extend the palms of their hands, which you will try to strike. Hit the invisible target lightly, as if it were the target.

For the jumping roundhouse, begin in a fighting stance. If kicking with the right leg, just prior to reaching the target, the left leg must rise up as high as possible for the extra power and the right leg scissors across in a round house kick to the target, striking with the ball of the foot, toes pointed down.

If using a roundhouse kick with the instep of the foot, be prepared for a little pain because of the sensitivity of the foot in this area. Keep toes flat with the instep, not bent up; this will prevent damage to the toes when performing this kick with the instep.

For a flying side kick over chairs, people, or even fire, start in a fighting stance. Run as fast as you can, as this will increase the height of the jump. If you run fast enough, you can climb high enough to extend in mid-air to a perfect side kick position, with a locked breaking leg. Locking the leg is very important to go through the target. As long as the leg is locked, there is no risk of injury to yourself. But if the leg is bent, and the target is not hit with a locked leg, the target exerting pressure back onto your leg might cause serious injury.

Look at your target while jumping. You cannot look anywhere else. You have a responsibility not to hurt your holders. You must have excellent reflexes, control and speed to absorb the pain. Do not hurt your fellow martial artists holding the targets for you. Shift sideways while jumping, if you have to, or lean down to land in between holders and helpers to avoid injuring them.

For split techniques, before jumping, practice the techniques with two target holders. Make sure they are positioned at the correct distance and height for your technique. Before running, adjust your steps to your target. When jumping, the left leg should be as high as possible before committing to the technique. Do not try to do split techniques without adjusting your steps and the distance between your targets. As you jump, extend the legs to a locked position and look at both targets. If you are breaking with a side kick, followed by a roundhouse kick, it is very important to develop speed and reflexes before attempting this break as one target must be struck while reaching for the other. Even if you lose your balance, still try. Maintain your position as high, strong and confident as possible.

If you are hesitant about breaking in public, practice privately after instruction about the correct technique by a higher belt. You may simply set up two cinder blocks, put pine boards across them (a half inch from each edge of the block) and try to break. The important thing is to try. By trying, you always succeed because no one can accomplish his ultimate if he does not begin by trying.

If family and friends attend a tournament or championship, ignore their presence. Do not think about what you did yesterday or what you will do tomorrow. Think only of the moment and the technique you are about to do. I cannot stress this enough. Always concentrate on what you are about to execute. This will help you achieve the best possible results. Concentrate on the moment; do not avoid it. Yet, don't be overly confident. If you miss on your first attempt, do not stop. Some people start slowly, others more quickly. Find your own individual style and pace. Each person has his own unique knowledge, skills, pace, techniques and abilities. It is up to you to develop your technique to its fullest potential.

Chapter 8

BREAKING, JUMPING AND FLYING TECHNIQUES

Flying Front Kick

Start from back stance facing the target. Take a few steps back. Run towards the target that is held up at your desired height. Remember you should try to practice several times. Jump straight up to the height you selected. Keep in mind the number of steps it took to approach the target to assure proper timing for the jump by picking up the back leg close to your body as high as possible. Immediately bring the kicking leg upward with your toes bent. Use ball of foot and snap it into target with focus, speed, strong yaa and power, then quickly bring down the kicking leg while in mid air to support your landing in a back stance.

Form Steps 1-7

1

2

3

4

5

6

7

Jumping Front Kick

a Set target with assistants at the proper height. Start with back stance approach target and determine how many steps are required before the jump to assure proper timing and distance.

b Push off kicking leg while picking up back leg close to the body as high as possible. Focus on center of target.

c Pull up your kicking leg (right leg) in a bent position and raise the knee towards the target. Thrust the ball of foot upward into target.

d After the break is completed, quickly withdraw right leg back to help with proper landing.

Flying Round House Kick

Repeat same as flying front kick and twist your hips while in mid air. Strike with kicking leg from outside angle into the target. The quick snap and the pivot of the hip will help you reach more height and an easy landing.

Flying Round House Kick

a Set up your target at selected height. Practice the jump to assure proper steps with good timing and extension.

b Approaching the target, pull up the kicking leg and raise it with great speed and power. Thrust leg with ball of foot greater than the target height to assure proper break in good timing. Quickly bring kicking leg back for good support on the landing.

Flying Side Kick

The most popular flying technique of all martial arts is the flying side kick. It requires coordination and good timing while running toward the target. While the body is flying in mid air, lift and twist the entire body side ways. Extend the kicking leg and cock back foot by kicking leg. Focus and tilt upper body towards the target at point of impact, snap kicking leg into the target, tuck your hands by your chest and extend lead hand along kicking leg. After thrust, quickly drop back leg to the floor to support the body for good landing.

Start with back stance, running toward the target. At jump starting point, lift your entire body as high as you can. Use the back leg for side kick and pull opposite leg up cocked to the knee of kicking leg. At this point, turn your body and hip side ways. Extend kicking leg out toward the target, snap thrust into target with strong yaa and lock your knee. Keep upper body forward and tuck hand by your chest. Quickly drop back leg to the floor to support the body for landing.

Form Steps 1-6

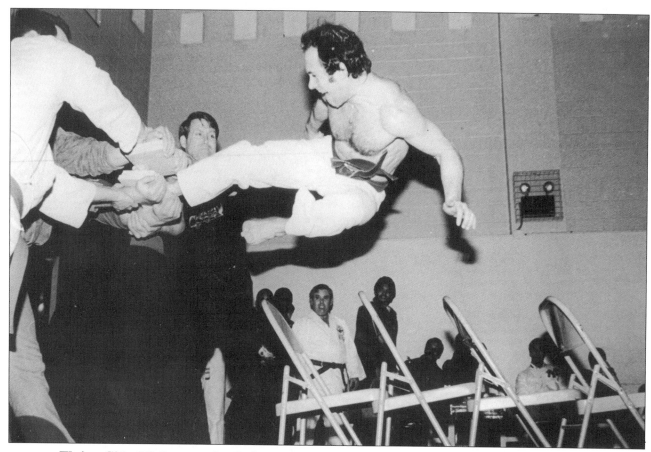

Flying Side Kick over six chairs. Breaking boards at 6 feet high (World Record)

Flying Side Kick

Double Legs Flying Side Kick

Repeat same as flying side kick. As you run toward the target, lift and jump in mid air. Turn the hip and the body, twist side ways at this point, extend both legs to a locked position. Focus the mind and coordinate all movements in good timing. While in mid air, thrust double legs into target. Quickly twist your back and land on your side with the hand extended close to the floor for extra support on landing.

Form Steps 1-6

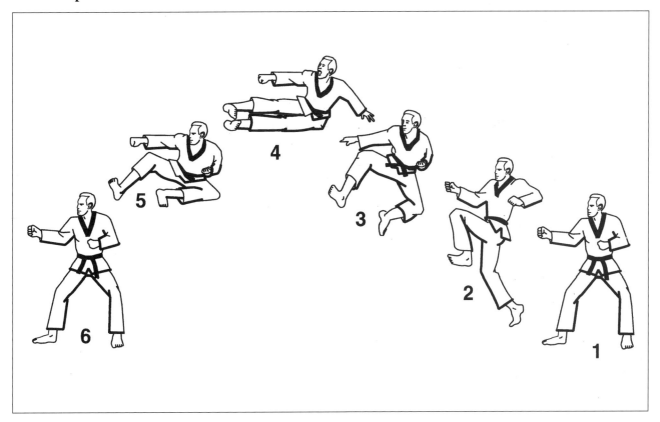

Double Legs Flying Side Kick

a Lift and jump in mid air. Twist your body side ways. Extend both legs and thrust into target. Focus on center with strong yaa. Make sure to see the target clearly without missing the target to avoid injury.

b After the thrust quickly twist your back, land on your side with the hand extended close to the floor for extra support on landing.

Applications

Focus on the target, extend both legs. Lock your knees and thrust into the opponent with strong yaa. Quickly extend your arm close to the floor and bring back both feet to landing position.

Flying Double Side Kick Practice

Striking the bag with both legs while in mid air. Good for fighting and breaking.

Flying Side Kick Breaking a 2x4

Breaking a 2x4 should rarely be attempted. It is very difficult to master, and it involves danger. **Only experienced black belt student should try this technique.**

The difficulty in executing this technique lies in the narrow target of the 2x4. While jumping with a side kick aim and twist your body and hip. Extend the kicking leg. Focus and thrust into the 2x4 utilizing all your body weight with all its power to successfully break. The target 2x4 has flexibility and you must penetrate in order not to be bounced back by its resistance. You must generate the power with positive mental attitude. Your mind must be under control without interruption. You must develop this kick by practicing on wall targets and focusing on one point so you don't miss on the break and injure your holders.

a Make sure to start with a distance of approximately 30' back from the target. Run with enough speed to help lift your body. At point of jump, focus on the 2x4; twist body side ways, and extend your kicking leg to center of the 2x4.

b Lock your kicking leg. Utilize your body weight for a successful break. Thrust into the target 2x4 with a strong yaa. Quickly after impact, bring back your cocked leg for proper landing on the floor.

Chapter 9

TRIPLE BREAK
And Advanced Breaking Head Break

Triple Break

Known as the most advanced breaking techniques that have inherent risks, difficulties in executions and even possible injuries, these breaks are performed for spectacular demonstrations. Students of the martial arts should have experience, focus and concentration. Practice the techniques over and over again in order to have good control. Timing, power, speed and most importantly perfection. Be ready to take risk and prepare yourself mentally with great confidence in order to avoid mistakes. If you use holders make sure to think about their safety and prepare them with an explanation with the lay out of the break step by step. Coordinate and rehearse with them before attempting the break.

a Strike with Triple Break
Set up your targets while holders adjust the height for each individual target. Practice the lift snap hands and legs while in mid air. Start again with proper distance before execution of break.

b Lift your body upward with both legs bent, toes curled up, ball of the foot facing target. Hand in position. Focus at center of targets.

c Thrust with speed and power into targets. Both hands and feet, elbows and knees should be in locked position

d Quickly after the thrust bring back both feet to landing position and place on the floor.

Application

e Strike against three opponents with hands to face area and kicks to stomach.

Jumping Split Leg technique in mid air with full leg extension.

Head Break

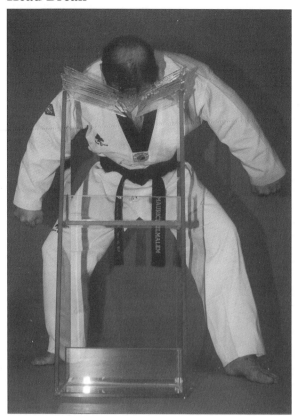

The head break can be risky and dangerous because of the brain location. When the head is used to thrust with speed and power into a solid target it can cause an immediate concussion to the brain that could include a weak and dizzy feeling. Depending on the amount of injury sometimes, as a result, you will have slurred speech or blurred vision for a short time and headaches.

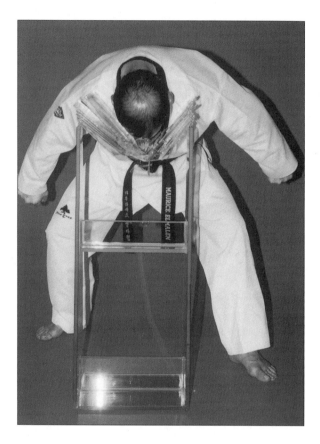

I do not recommend this break for anyone. It is to be done with extreme care. Use only top of the forehead with master timing when thrust. Never use the lower flat head section above the eyes due to the fragile bone fragments.

Speed Head Break (World Record)

Hold target with both hands directly in front of forehead. Practice the snap a couple of times back and forth. Connect the mind with your body when ready to execute the break. Start the forward thrust, aim at the center of the target with great speed and power and release the target in mid air. Snap the top of your head into the target with the help of your upper body pushing forward. Thrust the target with power and strong yaa to help absorb the pain and split the boards in half while in mid air. At point of impact release target to help the forehead extend through with great power.

a

a Hold target with both hands. Extend your arms to maximum forward in front of your face. Focus and concentrate on the target. Meditate for a few seconds and stay in front stance.

b Bring back target and place it by upper forehead to get the feel of the technique. Lock your back leg and hold the target firmly with your hands.

b

c

c Pre-select the angle to make contact with the upper top of forehead.

Speed Head Break (World Record)
A world record. Breaking five 1 inch boards while in mid air without any support or holders.

d Thrust target at center with great speed simultaneously bringing hands backward and snapping forehead forward. At point of impact, release target to help boards split in mid air.

Applications

a As opponent prepares to strike defender, quickly grab the back of opponent's head with both hands. Focus and aim with your forehead.

b Bring opponent's head toward you by pulling with your arms. Strike with snap of your forehead.

c Complete the strike with strong yaa and release your hands from the head grab.

Combination: Front and Side Kick

a

a Set up your target with proper distance. Use ball of the foot for front kick thrust.

b

b After you break with front kick, keep your kicking leg up and hold in cocked position while turning your head back. Thrust with side kick into target. Focus and good timing is important in all combination breaks.

c

c Application
Use front kick strike to the abdomen for the first opponent.

d

d Continue your defense with the side kick thrust without dropping the kicking leg, striking the rib of the second opponent disabling both opponents at the same time. You must use quick motions and reflex.

Combination: Round House Kick and Turning Back Hook Kick

a Place boards at proper distance. Try and check height by placing ball of striking foot at center of boards.

b Continue with turning back hook kick and place back of heel at center of boards. Do not over extend on the step forward when turning.

c Thrust with roundhouse kick into target using ball of foot.

d After breaking with roundhouse kick, continue with turning back hook kick making sure there is full view of the boards at time of thrust into target.

e Application against two opponents.
First opponent strikes with front kick. Defender counter attacks with round-house kick to chest area with right ball of foot.

f Defender continues with turning back hook kick to block second roundhouse kick.

a

b

c

d

e

f

Flying Side Kick Through Flaming Hoop

The experienced martial artist should always add new, innovative ideas using good imagination for all the exhibition techniques to keep himself on top and the audience waiting to watch more of the dramatic techniques performed with flair and style. Therefore, the flying side kick with the flaming hoop is the best example to demonstrate the difficulty of the technique by executing the side kick perfectly. The jump has to be timed right. The legs have to be tucked in with the body bent in order to be able to fit in the hoop while in mid air and at the same time twisting the body. Simultaneously extend the kicking leg and thrust into the target, ending with a safe landing. Most importantly do not touch the hoop of the fire. This element makes the technique extremely dangerous to perform.

The hoop should be comfortable and have a strong, sturdy base to prevent injury. Use a cloth around the frame of the hoop. To light it, use an ordinary lighter fluid like ronsonol (it burns itself out in few seconds) not gasoline. Practice the flying side kick through the hoop without fire. With the body tucked prior to entering the hoop, concentrate on twisting the body as it travels forward and do the side kick. Once you master this technique, flames should be added equally to control the intensity of the fire. The boards always should be visible and the kick should be well executed with proper focus at the center of the target. Do not hesitate to complete the technique from the start with full confidence.

a Start by placing the hoop of fire in the right place with holders away from the fire. Make sure of the distance (not too far from your reach). Holders must hold the target higher than the bottom of the hoop and at center. When jumping, tuck your legs and body so they can fit in the ring.

b Aim your kicking leg at center of the target. Make sure prior to the kick to jump high enough to allow for time on the extension of the side kick and the snap of the leg.

c Thrust the side kick into the target and lock your kicking leg to be able to go through the target. Prepare your tucked back leg and extend it for safe landing to reach the ground. Do not over extend your motion on the jump in order not to injure your holders by bringing back your kicking leg in position for landing together with the back leg. Avoid distraction and do not hesitate to complete the techniques.

Section VI

INTERVIEW QUESTIONS AND ANSWERS

Life is special to everyone, especially for those who benefit the most by achieving the dreams of life.

CHAPTER 1

Questions That Are Often Asked
by Magazines, Newspapers, Radio, and Television Reporters

I have had hundreds of interviews on television and radio and have been the subject of many magazine articles all over the world. Some of the most common questions are:

Question: Can you tell us what fighting and breaking means to you? How would you explain this to a student?

Answer: Fighting and breaking, in my opinion, is the ultimate challenge of one's ability. A martial artist must try for his or her personal best and show the results of his training. The ability to perform in championships carries over to life including work, family relationships and other personal best efforts. There is a time you must prove yourself. We face difficulties in life and we must pass through hard times. A good fighter will use his training and meditation to work through these times. Fighting is the preparation for an extreme challenge because the fighter must use all his personal skills learned throughout his martial arts training.

Breaking in martial arts training is the ability to break through a hard surface like wood, glass, ice, stones, etc. This ability allows me to show my ultimate techniques- the daredevil ones, which I invented. Breaking is the most fascinating aspect of martial arts next to fighting because of the challenge of putting yourself on the line in front of spectators. Misses are not understood in this venue! But, I love trying to impress spectators and earn their loud screams and clapping hands.

I am very thrilled at standing ovations after particularly risky breaks. So I choose the most difficult techniques to demonstrate. The audience enjoys this.

Question: How do you begin to practice for breaking and fighting?

Answer: I include knuckle, finger and palm push-ups to strengthen the triceps. The muscles used in push-ups give you the power for hand breaks. The makiwara board canvas that is made of hard foam is good for practicing punches. Use the first two knuckles of the hand to stiffen and break the nerves in that area so that you can numb the pain. Do this slowly and without excessive force. Strike various surfaces though, like punching bags, a bag of rice, or other hard surfaces such as wood and steel. Most importantly, progress to ever-harder surfaces.

I repeatedly push my hand in sand and rock salt as well as train on all kinds of hard materials. I use punching bags at all times to build up my speed as well as to stiffen up my knuckles. Sometimes, I even punch a wall for hard conditioning. For the legs, I use the ball of the foot to hit the punching bag, wall, even tree trunks.

One can also train the ball of the foot by hitting the floor. Make sure you bend your toes. The instep of the foot and heel can strike against the bag. Hitting targets imitates the motion of breaking. You can try different heights as well.

I would recommend to all students to practice these methods in school during class session while a master is present so that he can correct the angles of the strike. I also recommend young children not to do these training techniques. Juniors can start from age 12 to 15 and up. Under this age, kids are not fully developed mentally and physically to handle this pressure.

Question: How old were you when you started practicing martial arts?

Answer: I was 12 years old when I wanted to be a fighter and learned that if you don't have the combined power and speed or are not intelligent with your techniques, you can't hurt anyone. This realization all stemmed from a fight against a larger opponent. I had to force myself to get out of his sight by circling and by manipulating his mind so that I could penetrate his open target parts.

Question: When a student starts to practice martial arts you have suggested they can condition their hands. Do you have more suggestions as to how they can condition their legs for speed?

Answer: To train for kicking you must stretch 45 minutes to an hour and then work on your routine, your power and your precision. Many people have to learn to hit a target with focus, speed, and power, in different directions with different techniques.

Question: When you train do you hit at the target directly in front of it?

Answer: I look past the target, about a foot behind the target and go straight through instead of wondering whether it is going to break the surface or not.

Question: How do you condition yourself psychologically?

Answer: I go through mental imagery. I call it "bringing out the best". Every person has the best within himself. I must go inside my subconscious because broken boards and glasses have no life. So I must go beyond and into myself to find the energy in me.

Question: What targets should fighters and breakers practice on to improve their techniques?

Answer: They should punch a heavy bag to feel the contact. They should kick a well-mounted soft target, then progress to makiwara board to feel the power within themselves. From there they should proceed to boards. I do not recommend children or teenagers with undeveloped bone structures to try to break without the supervision of a master.

Hand targets are very important for fighting skills. That's where a student in martial arts, especially tae kwon do, has a chance to develop the speed and accuracy of necessary motions in all directions. Hand targets are designed to be used with another student holding the targets at the height desired by the practitioner. The targets have to be positioned in full view. This helps the martial artist develop accurate control and vision, as well as training the different circular motions of kicking and punching. Fighters can improve their speed within the combinations they choose, whether it is hand or leg technique. Hand techniques are one of the most important elements to practice in any martial art training.

Question: From your experience, is breaking or fighting for everyone?

Answer: No, not at all. Fighting or breaking is not for everyone. Breaking is striking something with no life or feeling that "hits you back". Many say they don't want to go through that pain, but going through the pain is what makes a good fighter or breaker. In fighting, many students do not want to face their opponents because of the fear that they might be defeated. They are afraid that they might be let down by not performing at their best. They are afraid to find out their weaknesses. That is a test of life. You are testing your ability to perform in front of a teacher or audience. By performing as a fighter, you take the chance at doing things right. This provides you with a life achievement. One develops confidence by taking chances. This process is true in breaking. Before you hit that surface, you are taking the chance of breaking your arm or leg or going successfully through it.

Question: What feeling do you experience when you break?

Answer: The thrill of a lifetime mission accomplished and a dream come through. You can't imagine the feeling at that moment it is great and importantly satisfying the excitement.

Question: When the target doesn't break do you think you stand a chance of hurting yourself badly?

Answer: Yes. When you put up whatever material you have and you miss, you can injure bones, nerves and muscles. You must know how and when to punch and strike. Body muscles react to hard targets if the opponent is well conditioned. Glass is like razor blades; it will cut badly.

Question: Could psychological injury result if you miss a break or lose a fight?

Answer: Yes. Psychological injury could occur which may result in one quitting martial arts altogether, or just quit breaking and/or fighting. Losing is a very big risk that martial arts practitioners take. When one loses in a fight, especially in front of family members, your master, fellow students or friends, I recommend meditation to allow psychological power to take over your mind and deal with the defeat. No one is made out of steel to go through life's hurdles without defeat. We all experience good and bad. We must learn to take it as it comes to us with a good attitude; then lifetime challenges become positive. That is how a good fighter or breaker pulls through bad experiences and goes on with life. Things always happen for which we are not mentally prepared. We do not face extraordinary circumstances everyday when our best ability must be performed. Sometimes, we make mistakes. What we should do with the mistake is to learn from it, practice, exercise and pull through. Strive to do better in the next contest or championship.

Question: When you practice your workout do you do it at a hundred percent, or do you only go a hundred percent during tournaments and championships?

Answer: There is an old saying "practice what you preach". When you are practicing your breaks in the dojo or gym, it has to be with the same attitude you have as on the day of any tournament or championship. You must train even harder when you are in the gym everyday than you perform in competition.

Question: How important is one's attitude during practice?

Answer: Without a positive attitude a student cannot progress in fighting or breaking because the power one must develop has to come from not only the technique but also the willingness to persevere. It will weaken you if you have a negative attitude. You might as well not participate when those moments occur.

Question: What do you suggest to your students to do technique-wise for their preparation to break with punches and sidekicks?

Answer: I tell them to view the entire body as a weapon. The punch or the kick involves the conditioning of all parts of the body. In tae kwon do, karate and other martial arts, the art involves the "empty" hand as well as the "empty" leg. There are no weapons. You are the weapon.

Question: Does the power of your strike come from inside yourself?

Answer: I have seen very strong men in my life, ones twice my size who cannot do what I can do. Inner power, that some men call the chiia or yaaa, some people call it chi, exists in different martial arts practitioners. But, whatever the name, inner power is mysterious and important to all martial artists. That is why focus and meditation is an important part of one's training. They generate power. In order to break or fight in a successful manner, one's energy has to be in full force. It is from inner power that we successfully proceed in pulling through the hurdles and the rough times in fighting or breaking even with the dangers posed by glass and other targets. Inner power comes from the soul and the heart. It comes out with a tensing of the abdomen and comes out with a loud yaaa. Focus is most important for this moment to occur and be successful.

Question: What age do you suggest kids should start breaking or fighting?

Answer: A young child shouldn't start breaking because the bone structure is not been fully developed. Age sixteen is appropriate for these activities. I see a lot of children out there breaking, but I think the boards have been doctored. Fighting is the opposite. I suggest children to start fighting at a very young age, 4 or 5 years old, because it enhances their minds' ability to think quickly and builds their reflexes. Both are good preparation for school education and outlook on life.

Question: Can "doctored" boards affect a child psychologically?

Answer: Of course. If a teacher fixes boards so they are more breakable than normal and the child breaks them in the dojo, the child thinks he is stronger than he is. In the street, everything is real. The child could overestimate his strength and possibly break bones. Not only to mention, the child could be psychologically damaged as well.

Question: Does a good breaker or fighter always look positively at the way they do things? Do you think the energy one must invest comes out of the martial artist or does the martial artist react to the demands of the situation?

Answer: When I break, I try to think of someone who has hurt my family or me. That attitude is then transferred towards the glass or boards I am breaking. It is the anger breaking, so I feel no pain.

Question: What do you do when you feel pain?

Answer: When I was younger in breaking and fighting, I reacted differently from the way I do now. Then I felt all the lumps and bumps. But I kept conditioning each part of my body I used to break and fight, which became like leather. The pain goes away more quickly and I heal faster than when I was younger.

Question: As a master breaker, what are the most exciting techniques you have mastered?

Answer: A technique that I feel is the deadliest break of all time is to break glass. No one in the history of the sport dared to break glass using the techniques that I have developed successfully. I have achieved six world records, which I have held for quite some time now. These record breaks include breaking 100 sheets of one-eighth-inch glass with a downward elbow strike. I have performed this break in front of an audience of Great Grand Masters and other world record holders on live TV Shows and in front of Guinness World Records representatives.

The second world record I hold is the knife hand shooto breaking of 50 sheets of one-eighth inch thick glass with a strike knife hand traveling through the fifty sheets of glass without losing a finger or cutting my hand.

The third is breaking five boards with a speed head break. I hold five one inch pine wood boards with my two hands and release the boards as I strike them with my forehead in midair and splice them in half. No one else has mastered these breaks.

Recently, on September 13, 2000 at Madison Square Garden, I performed in front of an audience which included the legendary movie star, Chuck Norris, Great Grand Master Aaron Banks, Grand Master S. Henry Chow, and Grand Master Dr. Richard Chun. I performed new techniques in an attempt to bring new life into the scene of breaking. I spliced a one-inch pine wood board in mid air with spear hand using my two index fingers. I also performed a thumb break. I held a one-inch board lit on fire with my left hand. I spliced the board in mid air as I released my left hand and broke it with my right thumb.

Other of my breaks are documented in Black Belt Magazine, Tae Kwon Do Magazine, Karate International, Action Martial Arts Magazine, and many other magazines including Inside Kung Fu. I have performed flying side kick breaks through a hoop lit on fire involving six boards. This technique involves a great deal of skill, as the threat of being burned is very real.

I have also executed a double flying side kick break simultaneously breaking six boards with each foot while in mid air. I have also broken five one-inch thick boards with a turning jumping back kick in mid air, splicing them in half. One of the most spectacular breaks that people like and I have achieved is the breaking of two by four. These world records brought me a great deal of personal satisfaction. I have been called the **"Houdini of Martial Arts."** Some reporters and Great Grand Masters of martial arts have even called me the **"World's Greatest Daredevil Champion"** of all time. Needless to say, I don't think my breaks are made for everyone to try!

Question: Try to describe one of your breaking routines during a championship.

Answer: A typical performance includes starting with a one-inch board spear hand break to impress the audience. That is a very difficult technique. I hold the board with my left hand and release it as I strike with the two middle fingers of the right open hand. I splice the board in half, in mid-air.

Once I gain the audience's attention, I go on to my head break. I break five boards speed-style. I hold the boards with both hands. At point of impact I release them and splice the boards in halves with my forehead.

Next, I do a flying technique breaking six one-inch boards with each foot and then flipping in mid air.

A typical sequence I include is a 2x4 break with a flying sidekick, 80 sheets of one-eighth inch glass break with a downwards elbow strike and five boards break with turning back kick..

Sometimes I will conclude my exhibition by breaking one-inch board lit on fire with my thumb. Holding it with my left arm, I strike the board with my thumb and break it in mid air.

Of course, I do not recommend many of these breaks for everyone. Many times I don't like to do what the crowd asks of me. Sometimes I demonstrate simpler breaks that demonstrate clean techniques. I am a very selective breaker. Brave stunts give me the courage to fight with full strength and include surprise and daring attacks against my opponents. Breaking gives me power and makes it easier to win.

Question: Please tell me about your famous punch, which is called "the ultimate one," the "bomb?"

Answer: Sure. A key technique in tae kwon do and karate is the reverse punch. This is a good technique for power breaks. At times, I will stack five or six one-inch boards. I will ask for volunteers to hold the boards. I focus and meditate before this power break for as long as it is allowed. For this break I have to use all my secret techniques to build the power in the body and mind to complete my right hand punch. The first two knuckles line up along the grain of the boards and break! Facing that many boards for this technique discourages many breakers. This ultimate punch is the one that brings respect to every martial artist who dares to try and execute this technique.

The execution must be so precise in perfectly combining speed with power. One must push the body and shoulders into the board. If you do not strike to break, you are ultimately taking a chance of breaking your arm, wrists and knuckles. The speed and yaa play a very important part in this break.

Focus is needed to punch with extreme ultimate power it takes to execute this break. One must pull the hand back as soon as possible after the break so that he does not push the nerves to that ultimate point where they just blow out and the hand is no longer in control. This is a very risky break and I have done it only three or four times in a major world championship to prove that power, combined with speed, as well as an ultimate reserve of nerves, brings success in this break.

The largest men do not own this type of break, size does make one more capable of executing this break. Regardless of who executes this break, the power necessary to do so, if used against an opponent's stomach, chest or ribs, will definitely paralyze him. But that is not what I am trying to do. I am merely demonstrating a technique and trying to make a good show.

Question: Maurice, are you in the Guinness Book of Records?

Answer: Definitely yes, I am in the Guinness Book of World Records. My records were broadcast live on television. I have been a champion for many years and many around the world including Great Grand Masters and world leaders have witnessed my breaks. My work has been documented in magazines, newspapers and books. I am most proud that I performed in front of Chuck Norris, Wesley Snipes, Burt Young, Carter Wong and the great Bruce Lee. Many people encourage me to continue demonstrating dangerous breaks and stunts. I still take new chances and challenges. Sometimes I have a very hard time going through with some stunts and I injure myself. But life goes on.

Long ago martial artists lived in the mountains. Students had to seek them out and ask them to teach them. Today, although I train alone a lot, I always ask my Grand Master, Dr. Richard Chun for advice.

I describe my proposed stunts and breaks, fully describing what I intend to do. He gives me the advice, do what my heart tells me to do, to be careful, and to go for it.

My records do not change me from continuing my other responsibilities in life. I wake up early in the morning (earlier than most) sometimes at 5 or 6 o'clock and work as late as 8 or 9pm. I earn my living in architectural general construction and building development. I always fit in my training. I go to my Grand Master's school several days a week and train as any other student trains.

It is a thrill to have done many TV shows such as David Letterman, ABC Wide World of Sports, Fox TV, Guinness World Records Prime Time, and many spectators have taken pictures of my outrageous breaks and stunts.

I am very thrilled that people take notice of me.

Question: What will it take to break your nerve and get you into a fight with someone?

Answer: I try to stay happy and calm, but once that is broken it is very hard to stop me. Once I am angry, it's very difficult to control. Also at a tournament, a black belt mistreated one of my students. I tried to talk it out but there was just no way of talking out of it, and he swung at me.

I will fight when the bell rings, but at that moment I could not resist the test. Therefore, this bigger man had to face me, things went out of control for no more than ten seconds before he was down. I felt very upset about it. It took fifteen guys to pull me off of him. I don't even remember, but it was said that guys were flying through the air because I threw them off me. As a result of that incident, I try even harder to keep cool and in control.

Question: What have you gained personally from your many years of training?

Answer: It has taught me self-defense, discipline and meditation. First of all, I learned how to protect myself mentally, physically, and spiritually. Many schools leave out the spiritual aspect of tae kwon do and martial arts.

I believe that is a very important aspect of training because this comes with a belief in God and the power that he put in us to protect ourselves. One's spirit gets one through death-defying fighting scenes and breaking challenges. The mental aspect of meditation allows us to go back to our roots when we were taught to be faithful and to follow good instruction. We all are students of God and we have to remember where we come from and what helped us grow. These remembrances push our thoughts from usual day-to-day thinking. Martial arts taught me to be a different person, thoughtful and smarter. I learned to observe, learn, watch, obey, pray, have faith and help others and not destroy. To be a good model of life.

Question: Do you think master fighters or breakers like yourself set a good example?

Answer: A martial artist cannot only break, fight with or without weapons, and do forms. A martial artist is an all-around person. You can't just be about the breaking aspect or the fighting aspect of this. You must judge the whole person that is the martial artist. Be a renegade man and share my ideas.

Before I became a master fighter or breaker, I was a student of all aspects of life. I injured many parts of my body, but it never stopped me. I am a now a world champion. As a breaker and fighter, I went into the extreme in myself and it brought out the best of me. But I derive personal satisfaction from not only the attention I receive as a martial artist but as a professional real estate developer, architectural designer, musician, artist and painter as well.

The martial arts are the most satisfying sport I ever became involved with and I am very happy I am still in the sport today.

Question: Do you believe that confidence improves one's fighting? Also, is speed and reflex training as well as strength training necessary to break and fight?

Answer: I believe that devotion and time put into practice and competition aid in breaking and in fighting. This strengthens techniques. The development of speed, reflex necessary to complete breaking techniques also increasing fighting ability to the extent of the time the martial artist puts into working out.

The work to improve fighting and breaking can be the same. As I have said many times earlier, speed is increased by working on the bag and wall targets as well as by jogging or jumping rope a few times a week. If one does not like jogging, he can swim. Swimming not only improves my speed but it relaxes me as well.

Other martial arts can also help one's specific martial art such as kick-boxing and kung fu, both of which help hand speed. I train how to fall. It is very important for a martial artist to know how to fall. It will avoid injuries such as breaking your head, elbow, knee and so on. In the street, for example, it is impossible to fight without the chance of getting hurt in some way, as there are no mats. The concrete will not absorb the fall. A fighter must know how to fall. This applies to a breaker as well when he does flying kicks. He must know how to tuck in his legs as they penetrate the board or whatever they are breaking while they are in mid air so that he can land safely. Landing the wrong way might break a hip, elbow, hand, head or spine. So I suggest that all martial artists learn how to fall at their school. Get instruction from a well-established master. I was taught how to fall by my Grand Masters side ways left hand extending parallel to the fall, hitting the buttocks first to absorb the fall and tapping the left hand on the floor first before extending and curving the back. Legs stay sideways. The same technique applies to falls on the right side of the body.

A front fall involves the extension of both hands, avoiding impact on the elbows and avoiding contact to the knees like a gymnast. Fall on the ball of the foot. Keep your head up so you will not break your nose or damage your face. There are many other falls such as the back fall, side falls, flips and so on. This helps a martial artist avoid injuries. Training properly for falls develops reflexes.

Question: Why did you want to become a martial artist?

Answer: It goes way back to when I was a kid. I witnessed many fights in Morocco, Israel and France. In those days, my father did not have enough money to enroll me in a private school to learn martial arts or gymnastics, so I had to begin on my own and learned street fighting to protect myself from kids who attacked me in school. I went on to search for the sport that would be most beneficial to me as self-defense and something I could enjoy.

That is how I fell in love with martial arts. Then there was the first class I attended in the U.S. I was not afraid to challenge the teacher who was conducting the class. When the Master approached me it became the most important moment in my life. The Grand Master asked me, "Do you know how to fight?" I did not hesitate. I said, "Yes sir, I will show you." At that point, my life was on the line. I did not know that I was facing a world champion named Joe Hayes or that the Grand Master was Dr. Richard Chun. I was 16 years old and alone in New York City. My family was living in Israel.

Suddenly, I was trying to fight this great world champion. His techniques flew right by me. Thank God, reflex took over. I blocked as many techniques as I could and fought back as well as I could. I got out of it alive and fortunately was not afraid. I did have confidence in myself and showed no fear in my fighting. Grand Master, Dr. Richard Chun, invited me to join his school. I am still his martial arts student and at the same school for the last thirty-three years.

I have had my own school as well and taught many students who graduated to be black belts. These students did very well in championships in the U.S. and around the world. I am very proud of that. I am delighted to write down my experiences and thoughts so that the next generation can learn from them. I still take chances and get involved in many aspects of martial arts such as traveling to Korea, France, England, Spain and Israel to participate in world championships. I wish for everyone to follow their dreams and accumulate experience, to look forward and never to stop because that is what survival in life is about.

Question: Is the reason you began tae kwon do for sports and educational reasons and not for revenge?

Answer: Yes, it was sportsmanship only. I do not look for revenge for anything. I try to reason with people as well as I can. I am a very humble man. I love the sportsmanship of tae kwon do. It became an Olympic sport in the Australian Olympics of 2000 and I am very proud to have been involved in two Olympic Games, Tae Kwon Do World Championships, two Macabia Games, etc.

I did participate in demos that encouraged the Olympic committee to consider tae kwon do a sport. I am very glad that they have reached this decision because many martial arts styles do not show the beautiful scquences of rapid kicking techniques and hand techniques of tae kwon do.

Question: Can you name some of the great masters you studied with?

Answer: I started to study martial arts with the world champion Gidon Kadari from Tel Aviv, Israel. He taught the basic fundamentals of martial arts. He was a shoducon stylist who actually studied Krav Maga the deadly combat karate for the Israeli military forces. He taught us many deadly secrets of martial arts and how to be ready for an attack at any moment. Also, he taught us to be humble. I do appreciate that approach, as there is no completely safe place on this planet. We can all strive to survive, but we have to learn to survive and that is all we can do.

Then I immigrated to the USA in 1970. I joined the Richard Chun Martial Arts Center. I became a very loyal student for many, many years.

I have also studied with the great Tiger Kim and Joe Hayes. I have learned kung fu fighting at the New York Kung Fu Academy. I tried wrestling in college as well as judo. I have developed special techniques in Krav Maga, the Israeli combat system but, of course, I have limited that to myself. I have taken many seminars with great fighters like Joe Lewis and Bill Wallace.

Question: What is the most valuable thing you receive from the Masters you studied with?

Answer: First, I learned respect. When one respects a master or teacher, he becomes your greatest source of information. In general, respect brings you closer to family, God and the world. Without respect, people tend to disregard you because they sense you do not appreciate your fellow man. Each and every one of the Masters has different ways and different techniques. They thinks differently. Martial artists reach the black belt level then begin the long journey to perfection of all the techniques. We must appreciate that we all think differently.

All martial art great grand legends have created different ways of utilizing their techniques. They come to these ways along a difficult path by experiencing the hard work of practice, practice, and practice. A great fighter can't learn just one technique; he must learn a variety of techniques. For example, if a fighter leads with his left hand to throw a jab at his opponent and injures himself, he must be able to continue the fight for his own respect with his right hand until the fight is stopped. A good fighter will not quit under any circumstances unless he is unable to commit to finish the fight.

This is a great lesson I learned. It is about survival. That is the pride we take in ourselves, do not give up to anyone. I have learned flexibility of approach. This is what meditation has taught me in martial arts-control of the mind. I learned to forgive evil parts in humans and to try to talk the opponent out of a fight. Meditation has taught me to take control of my mind and my body and not to work with anger towards life.

The philosophy of martial arts has taught me that everything is possible with the guidance of a Master who watches the progress of your dreams. Of course, the Masters have put in their time and effort to reach their legendary status. I respect that. I always have looked at great masters and legends with the highest authority because they were the example I followed and respected them. I have learned that I must be like a sponge whenever I encounter such a Master. In turn, I learned how to take care of others and help at all times. In being committed, I learn each and everyday that we must be willing to go back to the basics of martial arts. But, the routine is not always the same. As we progress, the techniques must be exercised in different motions, different speeds. All approaches must be executed with a positive attitude. That is what makes success.

I have had throughout my many years in martial arts the privilege of learning from my masters. I have listened to them, read their books and biographies, obeyed their orders, and thought about all the things that I have learned from them. I never found anything negative. It was all positive. A good master always leads and is the mentor to the students in the most positive way possible. I thank the masters I studied with for their efforts in teaching me what I know.

Question: Do you appreciate lightweight breakers or fighters and the special techniques that they can do?

Answer: Being a breaker has nothing to do with size. I have seen small guys who can break with the quality of larger men. It is the technique, not how big you are. The main things are speed, power, precision and accuracy. Sometimes people judge too quickly. My father warned me to see when I look at something. People sometimes are amazed when the little guy wins. It is the technique and the special elements that come with it, and not the size.

Question: That makes sense but do you have any suggestions for students when they train?

Answer: I train very hard to be the best and nothing less, because time lost is time lost and we must do the best while we can. The martial arts body should have all the nutrition that it needs: good food, good training program, and good diet.

A martial artist should respect himself at all times by watching his weight and by eating the right food. Mental outlook is what makes a martial artist. This is represented in the way one talks, dresses, acts, and conducts business.

Question: Do you have any idea where the art of breaking started?

Answer: Grand Master Masheo Yama was one of the greatest breakers in the world. There have probably been many great breakers before him, but he is the only one I heard of who stopped a ball with his own bare hands.

Question: Where did he come from?

Answer: Japan.

Question: Do you believe a breaker or a fighter when he succeeds at his techniques and wins championships it enables him to be mentally and emotionally prepared to meet other life challenges?

Answer: Like anything that you achieve, breaking makes your mind bolder. There is a song by the Temptations, "Standing On The Top". Everybody knows about you when you are on the top. I always try to stay on the top and acknowledge the ones on the bottom because you are going to meet the same faces coming down and going up.

Question: How does it feel to prepare for a championship?

Answer: While preparing for a championship, I put everything else aside and focus on the championship. When I am preparing to compete I put other activities aside, except those important to my championship. Other than the needs of my family, I put my affairs in order so I can focus. This is true for breaking and fighting. I rest well the night before, meditate and relax my mind, think of the best techniques and rehearse them in my mind.

Question: How many championships have you won?

Answer: I can't count them. I have over 700 trophies, 50 gold medals, 60 grand championships titles, 7 Time World Champion and still have the title 7 World Records and Guinness World Records, various "Hall of Fame" honors. I am thankful I won them. I worked hard to achieve these honors.

Question: Do you consider martial arts fighting and breaking an art?

Answer: Martial artists do train to protect themselves. We become weapons. One knows the pressure points of the body, how to take a man out and how to kill. A martial artist knows when they have won in the street or in a tournament. They acknowledge this point and leave the opponent alone. This is an art form. That's when the respect of humanity comes along. Respect of one another makes you a great fighter. Many of the great legendary fighters contribute to humanity at the end of their careers, whether it is through helping organizations or giving seminars or monetary contributions to the poor or creating programs to help the poor.

Question: Will you go to the aid of someone being attacked?

Answer: Yes, many times I myself might need help and with this attitude, I do help others. I have seen other people stand around and watch a crime being committed. Then, one day if it happens to them, they will want someone to help and only then will they understand this point. Everyone should help his fellow man. We should stand by each other and stop the crime if we can at that moment. It is a great challenge to subdue evil people.

Question: Are reflexes important in dangerous breaks, such as fire breaks, glass breaks, and flying techniques?

Answer: Of course. Reflexes don't matter if the mind is not energized. The mind must be conditioned so that the reflexes are helpful. Reflexes are only as good as the mind.

Question: What are the most exciting breaks you ever witnessed?

Answer: I saw many breakers in shows like the Oriental World of Self Defense, World Championships, Governor Cups, US Championships, and WTF Championships. I always see board and brick breaks mostly. The glass break in my opinion is one of the most dangerous and exciting breaks in martial art training. You must be very fast with glass techniques. You cannot waste any time. This speed translates well to fighting techniques. You can't think about it. You just do it.

Question: Where should a student try for a world record in breaking?

Answer: A student should choose a place where a large crowd will gather. Places like the Nassau Coliseum, USA, AAU World Championship, World Tae-Kwon-Do Championship, and Madison Square Garden are good choices. Also, a student should make sure great masters will witness the breaks.

Setting a world record is a very rewarding goal. It is a challenge that makes a dream come true. It brings good memories that stay with you forever, particularly if witnessed by great grand masters of the martial arts.

Question: What is your comment on breaking for those that are interested and have not tried to do so?

Answer: I would like to sum up that breaking is not for everyone. Although everyone can do it if they are trained properly and their mind is open to do it. I will suggest not to start breaking on your own, but only under supervision.

Question: When the muscles are strengthened and speed reflexes are developed, does the breaker automatically develop confidence?

Answer: A breaker, if his techniques are properly learned, will develop the confidence that he can hit someone and knock him out. A great breaker has the ability, strength, power, speed and confidence that he can hit someone and knock him or her out. This comes from the experience of hitting hard targets like bricks, boards, glass and so on.

Question: What are your thoughts to sum up your dreams?

Answer: Dreams are to keep us alive, motivated, and to make us happy for long life. They are the key to enjoyment and to staying healthy. Some artists know how to express their dreams in painting pictures or just building and putting them together. But in martial arts you learn to just do it. Try to overcome the obstacles in front of you. Take chances and see for yourself the outcome. Good or bad, it is reality that we must learn to deal with in our everyday life. Just do it. Be the best. We will know who we are. That is the spice of martial arts. Stay in shape and dream on for tomorrow. Stay focused and have peace of mind.

Chapter 2

GALLERY OF FIGHTING AND BREAKING DEMONSTRATION

CHAPTER 2

GALLERY OF FIGHTING AND BREAKING DEMONSTRATIONS

To present the most spectacular demonstrations students and masters of the martial arts must be very experienced in executing techniques with accuracy, speed, power, and most importantly, have the foundation for developing inner abilities to complement external accomplishments, take risks and follow through various stages of repetitions, self control, focus, coordination with holders, to be disciplined and to have an absolute confidence in himself. He must have the mind under control at all time of the demonstration. All targets should be selected carefully and positioned accurately with proper height and distance. Check holders for correct stances and the way they hold the target; if it is wood, along the line of grain. Meditate before striking. A martial artist should be creative and probably have a little showmanship in him with flair and style to attract the audience's attention. The more difficult and dangerous the break is, if executed properly, the more support you get from the audience; even a standing ovation. Demonstration programs in competition or in show must be kept fast moving, with innovative new ideas in order to stay on top. If you miss on your first break, try again. Sometimes distraction of the mind by being nervous can cause the miss. Trying to break on second time shows how difficult it is to break, and the audience will appreciate you more.

The author and publisher will not accept responsibility for any accident or injuries on the breaks demonstrated in this book.

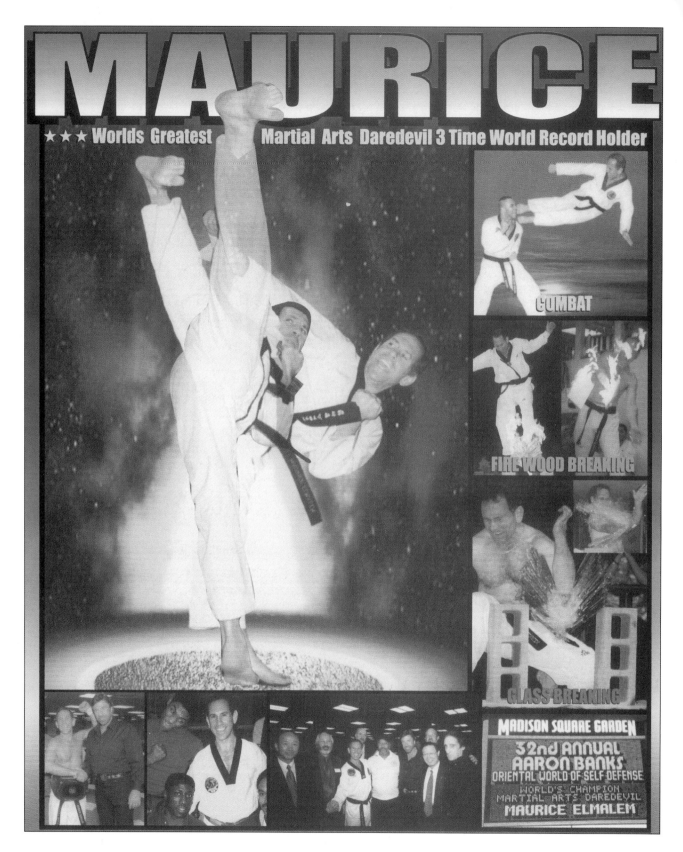

MAURICE

★★★ Worlds Greatest Martial Arts Daredevil 3 Time World Record Holder

COMBAT

FIRE WOOD BREAKING

GLASS BREAKING

MADISON SQUARE GARDEN
32nd ANNUAL
AARON BANKS
ORIENTAL WORLD OF SELF DEFENSE
WORLD'S CHAMPION
MARTIAL ARTS DAREDEVIL
MAURICE ELMALEM

• Master Maurice Elmalem with celebrities from bottom left. With movie star Chuck Norris receiving his 6th World title at Madison Square Garden. Next - movie stars Wesley Snipes & last Dragon Tamak.

• Next - Dr. Richard Chun, Rick Lanches, Maurice Elmalem, Rico Guy, Chuck Norris, Alan Goldberg, S. Henry Cho, Aaron Banks.

• **World Record** - Flying Double Side Kick with both legs simultaneously breaking five 1" boards while in mid air.

• High Flying Side Kick.

• **World Heavyweight Champion** - Ron Jeter using Elbow Strike Downward breaking seven 2" Cinder Blocks.

• Double High Flying Side Kick to face level.

• Master Maurice Elmalem in Seoul, Korea for special advance Tae Kwon Do training.

• The 11th World Tae Kwon Do Championships held at Madison Square Garden in New York City August 19-21, 1993.

• Spear hand thrust breaking 1" board with finger tips.

• Jr. Black Belt demonstration of high flying breaking techniques at the World Tae Kwon Do Championships. Madison Square Garden August 19, 1993.

• Back Flip Breaking Technique demonstration by members of the Korean Tiger.
Madison Square Garden August 19, 1993.

Chapter 3

CONCLUSION
Self Defense

Transforming Fighting and Breaking Techniques into Application for Self Defense.

The Habits of a Champion

A good fighter must be a good athlete - one who takes care of himself or herself. The training must be an all-around one. This training includes aerobic, anaerobic and sport specific training. A fighter should work on techniques and the basics that will make him a winner. This is not necessarily the fancy or showy techniques but basic ones. The goal should be to execute the break or score the point. In fighting, it is the simple techniques such as reverse punch, roundhouse kick, sidekick, or back kick that win.

To become a champion, one must be very well trained by Masters. The teacher does not necessarily have to be a champion. A lot of champions are not good teachers. Nor does one have to be a good fighter to teach fighting. A teacher just needs to have a point of view that is effective.

A great champion must ultimately rely on his reflexes. They are a big part of success, especially in fighting. A champion should train most days. Sometimes the body cannot take hard training without rest periods.

Competition is good for most of us. It transforms us. Modesty, courtesy and integrity must be kept as well as the desire to do better. One must learn the basics in martial arts and always remember them. It starts from the positions of the body to the thinking in our mind to gain the winning edge. Competition is not necessarily about winning or losing but about how one performs as an individual. All martial artists must have a positive attitude. This is the spirit of the martial arts. One who studies martial arts does so to learn, to win and lose with pride. As one knows more about the importance of energy, speed, and power, one can build oneself to be an outstanding martial artist.

One of the 50 Gold Medals won at World Championship Competitions

Knife Attack to Chest or Shoulder

a While attacker is in motion with striking knife hand quickly step out to the side with high knife hand block. Keep eyes focused on the knife.

b Swing attacker's hand in a wide circle then grab wrist with both hands.

c At completion of wide circular motion apply pressure with a twist to attacker's wrist.

d Continue applying pressure on attacker's wrist by swinging the arm forcing attacker to drop his body face down and release the knife. Stay focused at all times of defense.

Knife Attack Over Head or Face

a As attacker strikes with knife over head or face, use a high block and grab attacker's hand. Throw a punch to the rib to slow down the attacker's force.

b Keep blocking hands at grabbing position and swing attacker's arm to the side in a wide circle. Simultaneously grab the attacker's hand, bend the wrist and avoid touching the knife.

c Immediately step forward with back leg behind attacker's front foot while twisting the elbow forward and simultaneously sweep attacker's leg out, throwing him down.

d Keep a firm hold, twist the body and quickly apply pressure on elbow and wrist to disarm attacker.

Knife Attack To Face

a Focus on attacker at all times, control your mind and hold on to your nerves. Look directly into the attacker's eyes and on the knife. Use your reflexes and speed once the attack takes place.

b Take one step forward. Block attacker's hand with high block knife hand and stay focused on the knife.

c Swing blocking hand outward. Place your right hand under and around attacker's right hand with both hands in position.

d Grab attacker's wrist with left hand and place right hand by attacker's elbow together. Swing attacker's right hand downwards, pull up your right hand by the elbow with left hand pushing down until knife drops. This motion must be practiced slowly to avoid injuries.

Arms Grab Self Defense

a Attacker grabs both wrists from the behind.

b Turn slightly to the right in a circular motion inward, bring attacker's hands over head.

c Snap attacker's front leg with back leg. Cross hands over and twist them, creating pressure on the elbows to take down the attacker on his back.

d Use bottom of the heel to stomp on attacker's chest.

Defense Against Gun Attacker

a Focus on the gun. Use very fast motions to block attacker's hand.

b Grab attacker's wrist with left hand, snap on the elbow with right palm hand. Apply pressure by pushing palm hand upward grabbing left hand at the wrist downward. Keep face away from the gun and stay focused.

c Immediately throw a reverse punch to attacker's rib cage and keep a firm grip on attacker's arm.

d Bring attacker's arm with a twist, palm facing up. Keep the grip on the wrist, bring back hand and grab the arm. Simultaneously kick attacker's elbow with your right knee and push the arm downward with grabbing hands. Apply tremendous pressure to the elbow for the release of the gun.

Gun Attack to the Back of the Head

a As soon as you feel the gun touching the back of your head, don't panic. Focus and stay calm. Control your nerve and connect the mind with the body.

b Immediately turn right and with open right hand, block attacker's hand with the gun, push it to the side and upward to keep the gun away from your face.

c Quickly place left hand by attacker's arm close to the wrist and swing your right hand. Wrap it around attacker's wrist. Focus at all times. Keep the gun out of your face.

d With both hands, swing attacker's arm with a twist by creating pressure on the elbow and placing attacker's wrists with the gun at the stomach. Push the gun into the stomach to disarm attacker.

Defense Against a Mugger

a Act quickly with full control whenever attacker grabs your shoulder or any part of your body.

b Turn left and block attacker's hand with knife hand middle block. Be prepared for action.

c Push attacker away and kick with back leg using the knee to the stomach in full extension.

d After the knee kick, prepare to extend leg for front kick.

e Kick attacker to the groin with the extended leg to diminish him.

Defense Against Rape

a As soon as attacker grabs your neck, do not panic. Be prepared mentally and move quickly.

b Snap both open hands to attacker's ears to disturb his focus on the grab and cause him pain.

c Quickly as he lets loose of the grab, bring your right leg over attacker's right side and place it by the neck.

d Simultaneously, push attacker's head toward the floor with your right leg throwing him off balance while grabbing his right hand.

e Lock right leg against attacker's neck and pull his right arm in. Grab, lock and kick with left leg back of the heel to attacker's stomach.

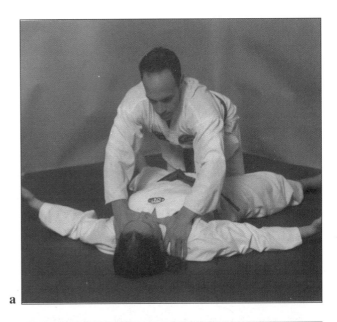

a

b

c

d

e

Defense Against Knife Strike in the Park

a Block attacker's knife hand with high block, throw reverse punch to rib cage to slow down attacker's motion and power. Stay focused at all times.

b Turn blocking hand outward with your left hand high block. Turn left and place attacker's arm on your left shoulder. To have complete control, use your right hand to grab the attacker's arm. Keep knife away to avoid injury.

c Place attacker's elbow on your left shoulder and to snap it forward.

d Push left shoulder upward against attacker's elbow and pull his hand downward, causing discomfort to attacker's elbow. Continue this motion until attacker is disarmed.

Defense Against Snatching Hand Bag

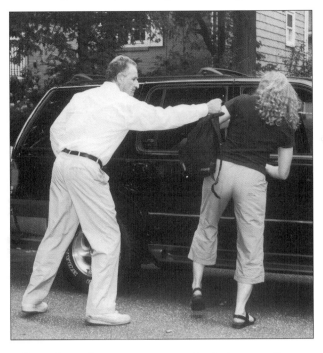

a Stay alert when you turn your back to open the car. A stranger is about to snatch your bag. Be careful.

b Respond by turning to your left grabbing the bag immediately and throwing a round house strike kick to attacker's chest area using power and speed so attacker will not have a chance to strike you back.

c Continue with second roundhouse kick strike to the face causing damage until attacker releases the bag.

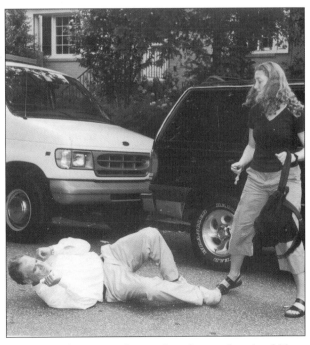

d With good strategy of execution, the attacker should lose his balance and fall to the pavement.

About the Author

Profile and Accomplishments

of

Greatest Martial Arts Daredevil

MAURICE ELMALEM is a Seven Time World Champion, 6th Dan Black belt with W.T.F. and 9th Dan Black belt with PWMAF. He holds Five World records and is a Seven Time U.S. Cup Gold Medalist and Four Time AAU Champion. He has studied the Martial Arts for 32 years under renowned Great Grand Masters such as Dr. Richard Chun, World Champion Joe Hays, Tiger Kim and Gidon Cadari. Maurice's fighting and breaking skills are documented and have been witnessed by millions on television, live shows at Madison Square Garden, Nassau Coliseum, Studio 54, Apollo Theatre and the Gleason Arena. Maurice has become a consummate martial artist. He credits discipline, hard work and dedication to his being the best. Winning with honor has made Elmalem a hero to both adults and children alike. Maurice is the "World Champion Greatest Martial Arts Daredevil" and has been featured in over 200 magazines and newspapers, has participated in over 750 Championships worldwide, and has accumulated over 700 trophies and 50 gold medals in fighting and breaking.

Maurice has been inducted into many Halls of Fame. He holds Seven World Records in breaking, splitting in half four 1" boards with speed head break, shattering 90 sheets of glass with an elbow strike, and 50 sheets of glass with a knife hand strike, breaking five 1" board with flying side kick over six chairs. Most boards broken simultaneously while in mid air with both feet "double flying side kick, breaking five boards with each leg while in mid air, won Maurice his 6th World Championship Title. His records are documented in the Guinness Book of World Records and have been broadcast live on Channel 5. Many who see Master Maurice look up to him and try to emulate him. They understand the discipline, hard work and commitment to excellence and to a dream required to master such feats. Maurice has perfected his art of breaking and transforming its potential to fighting and has become a master fighter. He is known as the "Greatest Martial Arts Daredevil." Guinness World Records Organization awarded him the title of "A Renaissance Man." He was nicknamed, "The Houdini of Martial Arts" in September 2000. After his performance in "Oriental World of Self-Defense" at Madison Square Garden, movie star Chuck Norris presented him with the world champion belt, which was engraved "World Extreme Daredevil Champion" and said to him, "You are a Great Champion."

The two most recent Guinness World Records held by Maurice Elmalem were established in 2001. He shattered 50 sheets of glass, amounting to $8^{1/2}$ inches of glass, with a karate chop at Fox Studios in Hollywood, California. It was televised on Fox Channels worldwide. In April 2002, Maurice established a new world record at Budo Martial Arts Magazine Studio in Madrid, Spain, breaking a hundred sheets of glass reaching to 13 inches high and in May 2003 Maurice established his seventh World Record at Palacio de Vistalegre in Madrid, Spain, breaking a hundred and five sheets of glass measuring $13^{5/8}$ inches high with one single elbow strike downward. With his outstanding grades in school and high IQ he achieved and experienced everything in life. He went on to become a musician and artist with 148 paintings. He is a sculptor, marathon runner, gymnast, acrobat, photographer, craftsman and real estate developer. He studied at Columbia University and New York University.

Maurice is listed several times in "Who's Who" in the East for outstanding contributions to Architectural Design, and he was voted among the Top 400 General Contractors in the U.S.A. by Engineering Report Magazine. His Motto is, "Work hard and go for the best, win and nothing less."

INDEX

Maurice Enterprise

Main Office:

684 Britton Street, Suite 4

Bronx, New York 10467

Tel (718) 652-7100   Fax (718) 652-6800

Email: mauricenterprise@aol.com

Website: www.mauricepromartialarts.com